Pub Quiz

Pub Quiz

Over 2500 questions for the best quiz night ever

ARCTURUS

ARCTURUS

This edition published in 2019 by Arcturus Publishing Limited
26/27 Bickels Yard, 151–153 Bermondsey Street,
London SE1 3HA

Copyright © Arcturus Holdings Limited

ISBN: 978-1-78950-975-5
AD005739NT

Printed in the UK

INTRODUCTION

You may want to use this book to challenge yourself on a wide range of subjects, or to pit your wits against your friends and family by setting up an informal, enjoyable quiz at home. However it is also the perfect resource if you're holding a more formal event, whether in a pub or elsewhere. We've put together some tips gained from years of experience to help you organize the perfect quiz night.

WHY HOLD A QUIZ NIGHT?

Quiz nights are very popular and are a good way to raise money for a charity or local project, with relatively little outlay on the part of the organizers; people have fun, while at the same time donating to a good cause.

Moreover, people can, with very little persuasion, add to the funds raised by buying raffle tickets, or paying a nominal amount to enter supplementary competitions during the course of the main quiz, and these supplementary competitions are seen to add variety and amusement to the event.

PLANNING THE NIGHT

Think about the purpose of the quiz, and aim to involve the charity or project concerned by inviting representatives along to give a short speech of thanks at the end of the evening – after all, the participants have given of their time and money, and it is nice to be able to reward them with an acknowledgment of their donation.

WHO ARE THE PARTICIPANTS?

Are they adults, children, or a mixture of both? Is the venue suitable for the ages of the participants?

Most quiz nights are aimed at an adult audience, because of the nature of the questions, or the time of the evening at which the quiz finishes, or the location (a public house is a popular place for a quiz, but not suitable if children will be attending).

WHERE WILL THE QUIZ TAKE PLACE?

How many people are likely to attend and how many can the venue hold? Is the venue easy to reach by car, or public transport? Are there parking facilities?

WHEN WILL THE QUIZ TAKE PLACE?

Consider who will be attending the quiz: are they mainly young or old, working or not working, or will there be a combination of these? Starting too early in the evening may dissuade some people; and starting or finishing too late may dissuade others.

Generally, a quiz night will start at either 7.30pm or 8.00pm, with participants being asked to arrive half an hour before the start, in order to allow time for them to find a table, write their names onto answer sheets, provide themselves with food, drinks, raffle tickets, etc, take a comfort break, visit the bar, etc; and generally do what people do before the start of an event.

If you are selling raffle tickets, then you also need to allow time for the participants to view the prizes and buy tickets.

Think also about the day and date of the event. Many people will not attend if they are working the next day, so Friday or Saturday evening is generally best.

Try to find out if there are other events in the neighbourhood on that date, which might conflict with your quiz night. If a date near to Christmas, or one which clashes with a major sporting event is chosen, then this might also result in lower attendance numbers.

WILL HELP BE NEEDED?

It is very hard for just one person to run a quiz night, so it's a good idea to have a group of helpers lined up for the night.

Perhaps you have decided to sell tickets to the event, or perhaps an entrance fee will be charged at the door – who is going to collect the money?

Will there be a prize for the winning team or each member of the winning team? Will there be a grand raffle? If so, who is going to provide the prizes?

Many retailers (especially on learning that the quiz is being run in aid of a charity or local project) will donate a small prize or two, and individuals taking part in the quiz can be asked to bring along a small prize on the evening itself, particularly if you tell them that this could be something they received as an unwanted birthday or Christmas present!

If you are running the event for a charity, they may have a pool of prizes previously donated for raffles, from which they could draw a few things for your own raffle.

Of course, if you are lucky enough to attract too many prizes, you can also hold an auction at the end of the evening, or hold onto some of the prizes for your next quiz night.

HOW MUCH TO CHARGE

This can be a tricky one, because at the outset, if you have not run a quiz before, or there has not been one in the area, people may wonder what is involved.

Flyers (mini advertisements) given out before the event will give people an indication of what to expect to pay for entrance and participation, but if you are in doubt, charge a minimal amount for the entrance fee, and try to make a little more money on other games and raffles during the evening.

Once people are accustomed to your quiz nights, however, you will probably find that they are willing to pay a little more: after all, they are getting a whole evening's entertainment for a relatively small charge.

Another factor to consider is that people may want supper. If you intend to provide supper, you would be well advised to issue tickets for the event, so that you are sure of covering your costs with regard to food. A light buffet could be provided; a venue will sometimes offer basket meals for a small price; a local take-away could be persuaded to come and take orders: if you sell tickets, you could include a take-away supper in the price, and this gives the caterer advance notice of how many suppers are required.

DRINKS AND SNACKS

Unless your venue has catering facilities, you may need to think about providing a range of drinks and snacks, as people are likely to get thirsty or peckish as the evening wears on.

If you are providing drinks or snacks, make sure that you adhere to any laws (national or local) regarding the sale of food and drink (particularly alcohol).

CAN YOU BE HEARD?

When the room is full, and people are chatting, it is often difficult for those participants furthest away from the question-master to hear what is being said.

You may need to hire a microphone and amplifier for the evening; if this is the case, then be sure to try it out a few days before, to make sure it is working correctly.

INSURANCE AND PUBLIC LIABILITY

Another factor to take into consideration is insurance: is the venue's insurance cover up-to-date and will it cover such an event, including members of the public and all other people who will attend, plus helpers and yourself?

You have a duty of care to the public, and must make sure that the venue is safe.

If you are in any way unsure, speak to an insurance broker, who will be best placed to give you all the advice you need, and to answer your questions.

Do you need any public entertainment permissions, or any other permissions? If you intend to play any music, etc, make sure that the venue has the required permission(s): on balance, it may be a good idea to avoid music altogether, as it is often not worth it just for one evening.

PUBLICITY

Do remember to publicize your event, as well as informing people verbally.

Put posters on noticeboards, or ask shopkeepers if they would be willing to display one in a window: who knows, they may even sell a few tickets for you, too! Try to get a mention of the event in the media if you can, but bear in mind the limitations of the venue: if too many people turn up, you may not have room for them.

SUPPLIES CHECKLIST

Apart from raffle tickets, raffle prizes, tickets, flyers and advertisements, and a microphone and amplifier, there are a few other things to think about: answer sheets for the participants to fill in the answers to the quiz questions, scrap paper for the participants, supplementary competitions, etc.

It is a good idea to provide each table with several scraps of plain paper, on which people can write ideas and show them around, as team members will not want other people to hear a discussion they are having about a possible answer to a question. And it is surprising how many people will arrive at the quiz night without a pen, so it's a good idea to have some spares!

You will also need a float, that is some money that can be given as change to people who pay for entrance, raffle tickets, etc. Make sure that you have sufficient funds, as nothing is worse than having to write an IOU or trying to keep account of what is owed.

TIME YOURSELF

Try out a few quizzes, to see how long it takes to read each question, giving the participants sufficient time to fill in an answer (and allowing sufficient time at the end for anyone who didn't hear a particular question to have it read out again). Now add on five minutes, which allows for teams ask for questions to be repeated, to complete their forms, and to pass their answers to a another table for the scoring.

After each round, the question-master reads out the answers, and the teams score them: the usual number of points being two for a correct answer and one for an answer which is 'near enough correct'. A 'near enough correct' answer is, for example, one which is misspelled, or one where a name is requested, but the answer just gives the surname, as opposed to the full name required for two points. You can use your judgment on this, should any scorer raise the matter, or when checking the answer sheets after they are handed in for marking on the scoreboard.

Having decided how much time to allocate for each round, plus form passing, plus answers, multiply that time by the number of rounds you intend to have, and then add a few minutes.

It is better to allow too much time than too little, as any spare time can be filled with an interval (for comfort breaks, trips to the bar, etc), or for playing a game or holding a supplementary competition.

If supper is to be served, then time will need to be allowed for this, too.

You will also need time at the end of the evening for the presentation of prizes, the drawing of the raffle, a speech of thanks, and for people to get their coats on, prior to the close of the venue.

It is usual to have eight rounds of questions per quiz night, but if time is short, then this can be cut back to five or six rounds (just remember to alter the scoreboard to suit). Choose the subjects of your rounds carefully, making sure you pick rounds on a good variety of topics.

SCORING

Thinking of the scoreboard, it is a good idea to have a flip-chart, with a large piece of paper, on which the numbers of teams, as well as the individual quiz round numbers, have been written, so that teams can see how well they are doing compared to others. Here is an example:

Team	Round Number								Total Score
	1	2	3	4	5	6	7	8	
1									
2									
3									
4									
5									
6									
7									
8									
9									
10									
11									
12									

Do prepare this chart in advance of the night of the quiz, as it will save time. You won't necessarily know the teams' names before the night, of course, but remember to leave enough room to write in each name below the team number: some can be quite lengthy! Teams are encouraged to give themselves a name in addition to their number, as this adds to the fun: 'Universally Challenged' and 'Littlehaven Lounge Lizards' are a couple of names recently seen at quiz nights.

How many in a team? Between three and six is typical, but if individuals turn up on the night, then it is usual for the organizer to sit them at a particular table that has been set aside for the purpose of later matching them up with other individuals.

ON THE NIGHT

Aim to arrive about an hour before the quiz starts, in order to leave enough time to set up the tables and chairs, and to arrange the quiz-master's table and sound system, the entrance table (at which money or tickets for entry are taken), the scoreboard, the raffle table, etc, as well as put answer sheets, pens, and scrap paper onto the tables which will be used by the participants.

At the start of the quiz, explain that there are several rounds and then ask each round of questions in the way you practised when timing yourself.

While you are asking the first round of questions, the scorer will have time to mark up the scoreboard with the name of each team.

After each round, ask each team to pass their answer sheet to another team for scoring purposes, then to hand it to the scorer for marking on the scoreboard.

Half way through the rounds, you might choose to have a break, either for supper, or to allow people to fetch drinks perhaps: it is entirely up to you how many breaks you include in the evening, as this depends on the amount of time available.

After all of the quiz rounds are complete, it's time to total the scores and announce the winning team (presenting them with a small prize, if desired), draw the raffle, announce the winner(s) of any other competition(s), and thank the teams and the helpers for taking part in raising money.

By now you should have a rough idea of how much money has been raised by entrance fees, raffle, competitions, etc, and your audience will be keen to learn of the amount, even if you cannot give them a precise figure.

AND FINALLY...

Give everyone details of your next Quiz Night!

ROUNDS

General Knowledge

1 In which part of the human body are the calcaneus, talus and navicular bones?

2 The location of a particularly barbarous French prison until its closure in the 1950s, Devil's Island is in which ocean?

3 Which was the last of the ten plagues of Egypt, as described in the Bible, in Exodus, Chapter 11?

4 Which capital city is served by Queen Alia International Airport?

5 The game of Scrabble (trademark) is played on a board with a total of how many squares?

6 The element of water is associated with which three signs of the zodiac?

7 What appears in the centre of the flag of the Republic of Ghana?

8 What is studied by a dendrologist?

9 Which two countries border Bangladesh?

10 Which Roman god of doorways and passages is depicted with two faces on opposite sides of his head?

Fruits 'n' Nuts

1   What kind of fruit is a canteloupe?

_____

2   Where in the mid-Atlantic can you find tropical fruits grown in hothouses heated by natural sources?

_____

3   The frying medium, groundnut oil, is produced from which kind of nut?

_____

4   The clementine is a cross between which two citrus fruits?

_____

5   What is the common name for the fruit, 'prunus persica'?

_____

6   Which South American country produces the most Brazil nuts?

_____

7   What is the more common name for the citrus fruit, the shaddock?

_____

8   'Cherry', 'Plum' and 'Grape' are all varieties of which fruit eaten as a vegetable?

_____

9   Which fruits grow on the 'malus' tree?

_____

10   What is a drupe?

Sport

1. Who won the British Motor Racing Grand Prix in four consecutive years during the 1960s?

2. Which Australian tennis ace holds, as of 2013, the greatest number of singles titles?

3. Which female German swimmer won a record six gold medals at the 1988 Seoul Olympics?

4. Which former U.S. baseball player gets a mention on the Simon and Garfunkel song 'Mrs Robinson'?

5. The English Channel was first swum in 1875; by whom?

6. What nationality was Andres Escobar, a football player shot dead in reprisal for scoring an own-goal in 1994?

7. 'The Iron Horse' was the nickname of which American baseball ace?

8. The Arthur Ashe tennis stadium stands in which U.S. city?

9. In gymnastics what is an alternative name for a backward handspring?

10. As of 2013, which boxer was the only heavyweight to remain undefeated throughout his career?

Travel and Transport

1. What on a ship is a jib?

2. Who invented the internal combustion engine?

3. What A is the national airline of Russia, code name SU?

4. Which German airship exploded in New Jersey in 1937?

5. By what popular name was the Boeing B-17 bomber known?

6. Charles Lindbergh made the first solo, non-stop flight across which ocean in 1927?

7. In which Italian city is the 'gondola' a popular form of transport?

8. Which German engineer founded a motor car company in 1890 which later merged with the Benz Company?

9. Which British travel agent organized his first excursion, a train journey from Leicester to Loughborough, in 1841?

10. In the early part of the 20th century, the 'Olympic' was the sister ship of which famous White Star liner?

Religion

1 In the Christian calendar, what name is given to the twelfth day after Christmas?

2 Who was the founder of the religious sect 'The Plymouth Brethren'?

3 Into what state do 'just souls' go, when they are barred from heaven through not being baptized?

4 What is the name of the river sacred to Hindus?

5 The colony of Pennsylvania was founded by which Quaker in 1681?

6 Which black American baptist minister won the 1964 Nobel Peace Prize?

7 Which Italian town is said to contain the home of the Virgin Mary, carried by angels from Nazareth?

8 Which Christian organization was founded by William Booth in 1865?

9 Followers of which Celtic religion regarded the oak tree as sacred?

10 Which city in Saudi Arabia is the birthplace of Muhammad?

Language

1 The name of which month of the year means (in Latin) the month of purification?

2 What 'ology' is concerned with the study of unidentified flying objects?

3 What is musophobia the fear of?

4 Aerophobia is a fear of flying, agoraphobia is a fear of open spaces, what is acrophobia a fear of?

5 It's Afrikaans name is Kaapstad. By what name do we know this South African city?

6 Uluru is the aborigine name for which famous Australian landmark?

7 To a male Australian, what are his 'strides'?

8 If ursine means 'bear-like' or relating to bears, what animal does hircine refer to?

9 In computing, how is a modulator-demodulator more commonly known?

10 From the French for 'knee breeches', what name is given to women's knee-length trousers, cut with very full legs to resemble a skirt?

Geography

1 Which American mountain range contains the Yosemite National Park?

2 Which American river is the chief tributary of the Mississippi?

3 Of which country is the Sierra Madre the main mountain system?

4 Where in the U.S. would you find the inscription: "Give me your tired, your poor; your huddled masses; yearning to breathe free"?

5 Of which African country is Bujumbura the capital?

6 Of which U.S. state is Lincoln the capital?

7 In which U.S. state is the city of Grand Rapids?

8 Of which ocean is the Coral Sea a section?

9 Of which U.S. state is Providence the capital?

10 Which British crown colony occupies a tiny peninsula at the southern tip of Spain?

Classical Music

1 Who composed 'Wellington's Victory'?

_____

2 What is a 'chorist'?

_____

3 The 2nd movement of J.S. Bach's 'Orchestral Suite No. 3 in D', is better known as ... what?

_____

4 What was the name of the Italian family, other than Stradivari and Guarnari, who made Cremona famous as a center of violin making in 16th-18th centuries?

_____

5 The Spanish 'Ritual Fire Dance' comes from which ballet with songs by Manuel De Falla?

_____

6 The 2nd movement of the 'String Quartet No 1 in D' by Tchaikovsky is better known as ... what?

_____

7 'Anitra's Dance' is part of the incidental music written by Grieg for the poetic play by Ibsen, called ___?

_____

8 What does the instruction 'alla moderna' mean?

_____

9 What piece of classical music was used as the theme tune for TV's 'The Lone Ranger'?

_____

10 Who composed the 'Ride of the Valkyries'?

General Knowledge

1 Which drink, still very popular today, more than a hundred years after its invention, was the brainchild of American pharmacist Caleb Bradham?

_____

2 What is the name of the very popular resin-flavoured white or rose wine of Greece?

_____

3 The notorious prison camp at Guantanamo Bay is located on which Caribbean island?

_____

4 What kind of animal was the tarpan, thought to have been rendered extinct in the early 20th century?

_____

5 In a symphony orchestra, the stringed instruments (excluding harps) are divided into five sections: violins 1 and 2, violas, cellos, and which other?

_____

6 Which year saw the start of the French Revolution?

_____

7 The first large-scale production of canned foods started in 1810, but there was one main problem: what was it?

_____

8 Bananas contain a moderate amount of manganese and a high amount of which other trace metal?

_____

9 With around 2.2 million people in its prisons in 2014, which country has by far the world's largest prison population?

_____

10 From which country did Algeria gain independence in 1962?

Movies

1 Which British actress played Lenny Weinribb's wife in the Woody Allen movie 'Mighty Aphrodite'?

2 Who starred as the aging football star prematurely summoned to judgement in the movie 'Heaven Can Wait'?

3 In which 2000 movie did Meg Ryan, Diane Keaton and Lisa Kudrow star as the daughters of a dying father, played by Walter Matthau?

4 Which actor played the wheelchair-bound Man With A Plan in the movie 'Things To Do In Denver When You're Dead'?

5 Who won a Best Actor Oscar for his performance in the 1975 movie 'One Flew Over the Cuckoo's Nest'?

6 Which actor was both one of 'The Dirty Dozen' and 'The Magnificent Seven'?

7 The movie 'Sleepy Hollow', took its name from the novel 'The Legend of Sleepy Hollow', by which writer?

8 In which movie does Clint Eastwood play a disc jockey harassed by a disturbed fan?

9 What kind of aquatic creature killed John Wayne in the 1943 movie 'Reap the Wild Wind'?

10 Who was the father of Luke Skywalker in the 'Star Wars' movie?

The Animal Kingdom

1 Which wild dog of Central and North America is also known as a prairie wolf?

_____

2 Which large American frog can jump up to two metres?

_____

3 Which large water bird has a pouch underneath its long bill in which it stores fish?

_____

4 The Sea Elephant is the largest of what type of creature?

_____

5 The peregrine is a type of which bird?

_____

6 What bird is a merganser a type of?

_____

7 What are salmon called during the first two years of their life?

_____

8 What are the main respiratory organs of fishes and many aquatic animals?

_____

9 What type of creature is a Portuguese man-of-war?

_____

10 Which nocturnal beetle is also known as the 'glow-worm' or 'lightning bug'?

History

1. In which year was the Cuban Missile Crisis, when the U.S.A. and U.S.S.R. almost started World War Three?

2. The Battles of Balaklava and Inkerman were fought during which war?

3. After it was destroyed by German bombers in 1940, which English cathedral was rebuilt and reconsecrated in 1962?

4. Which two countries, apart from Britain, defeated Napoleon at the Battle of Waterloo?

5. Who was the father of Elizabeth the First of England?

6. Who did James Earl Ray assassinate in April 1968?

7. Albert Einstein famously said that only two things were infinite; one was the universe, what was the other?

8. Of the Seven Wonders of the Ancient World, what is unique about the Great Pyramid of Giza?

9. In which present-day European country was the Lombard Kingdom founded in the sixth century?

10. Destroyed by a giant tsunami around 1500 B.C., on which Greek island was the Minoan civilization based?

General Knowledge

1 Which lower level of clouds are commonly called 'rain clouds'?

_____

2 Which American university is in Newhaven, Connecticut?

_____

3 What is the name given to the equinox which occurs around 21st June?

_____

4 What is the English name for the Swedish city of Göteborg?

_____

5 What name is given to violent circular storms in the China Seas?

_____

6 Which branch of mathematics deals with the relation of angles and sides of triangles to one another?

_____

7 What is another more common name for a Gazelle Hound, which is believed to be one of the breeds Noah collected into the Ark?

_____

8 What hot, parching wind blows from the Sahara in a northerly direction over the Mediterranean and Southern Europe?

_____

9 Which is the largest member of the dog family?

_____

10 What, to a Native American, is a calumet?

Art

1. Which French Impressionist artist was famous for his many paintings of water-lilies?

2. Which English artist was famous for his bleak industrial landscapes featuring matchstick figures?

3. Which French artist painted 'Olympia' and 'Le Déjeuner sur l'herbe'?

4. With which branch of the arts was Robert Mapplethorpe chiefly associated?

5. Which Dutch Post-Impressionist painter cut off part of his left ear?

6. What name is given to a painting or sculpture of Christ crowned with thorns, from the Latin for 'Behold the man'?

7. Who painted 'Impression: Sunrise' that gave its name to the Impressionist movement?

8. Which wood carver and sculptor is best known for the choir stalls and organ screen in London's St Paul's Cathedral?

9. Andy Warhol became known for his colourful reproductions of everyday objects, such as which brand of canned soup tins?

10. Who was the Italian renaissance painter whose works include 'La Donna Valeta' and 'The Marriage of the Virgin'?

Literature

1 Who is credited with the authorship of the fable 'The Tortoise and the Hare'?

2 What were the first names of the two brothers Grimm, famous for their fairy tales?

3 What is the name of Don Quixote's squire in Cervantes' novel?

4 What is the first name of Agatha Christie's Miss Marple?

5 Which German author wrote the short novel 'Death in Venice'?

6 Who wrote the horror novel 'Dracula'?

7 Which U.S. 'Beat movement' author wrote 'On The Road' and 'Big Sur'?

8 Which French author wrote 'Les Enfants Terribles'?

9 What was the first name of Sherlock Holmes's friend Dr. Watson?

10 Which British novelist wrote 'Our Man in Havana'?

Politics

1 Which European monarch abdicated on 2nd June 2014?

2 What does the W in George W. Bush stand for?

3 In 1819, from which country did the U.S.A. obtain the land now known as Florida?

4 Who was president of Chile from 1973 until 1990?

5 Zulfikar Ali Bhutto and his daughter, Benazir, have both been prime ministers of which country?

6 Who was the first president of Israel?

7 Which European country restored its monarchy in 1975?

8 In which American city in 1999 were demonstrators involved in violent protests during meetings of the World Trade Organization?

9 Of which Asian country was Cory Aquino the president from 1986 to 1992?

10 What kind of creature was Benito Mussolini's pet, Italia Bella, which travelled around with him?

Rulers and Leaders

1. Of which South American country was Pedro I the first emperor?

2. Of which country was Carol II king from 1930 to 1940?

3. Jimmu was the legendary first leader of which Asian country?

4. The Incas were the hereditary rulers of which South American country?

5. What title was formerly given to the Emperors of Germany and Austria?

6. What name was given to the forces organized in London by General de Gaulle during the Second World War?

7. Which Roman soldier and politician was a member of the First Triumvirate with Julius Caesar and Crassus?

8. Who was the leader of the Khmer Rouge whose death was announced in April 1998?

9. Hapsburg was the name of the former royal family of which European country?

10. Which U.S. cavalry regiment did Custer lead to disaster at the Little Bighorn?

General Knowledge

1 Before the Euro what was the former currency unit of The Netherlands?

2 What type of flowering garden plant originated from Mexico and includes the varieties ball and collerette?

3 Memphis was the ancient capital of which country?

4 In which year of the 20th century did America celebrate its Bicentennial?

5 The name of which North African city literally means 'white house'?

6 Who died after being shot whilst watching a performance of the play, 'Our American Cousin', in 1865?

7 DKNY is a well known designer fashion label. What does DKNY stand for?

8 What are the first names of Elvis Presley's daughter?

9 In the world of computing and the world wide web, what does ISP stand for?

10 Shades of which colour can be described as cobalt and Prussian?

Airports

1 Which U.S. city is served by Bob Hope Airport?

_____

2 How was Liverpool's Speke Airport renamed in 2002?

_____

3 Which European capital city is served by Arlanda Airport?

_____

4 What was the former name of New York's John F Kennedy Airport?

_____

5 Johannesburg International Airport was originally named after which South African statesman?

_____

6 Keflavik is the main international airport of which country?

_____

7 Linate and Malpensa airports serve which Italian city?

_____

8 Which U.S. city is served by George Bush Intercontinental?

_____

9 The airports of which country all have Y as the first letter of their three-letter codes?

_____

10 Handling over 66.4 million passengers in 2013, which is the world's busiest airport?

Mythology

1. Which Greek god was known in Roman mythology as Bacchus?

2. Which legendary Greek poet and musician attempted to rescue his wife Eurydice from Hades?

3. Who was the god of the dead in Egyptian mythology?

4. In Greek mythology, what creatures formed the hair of the Gorgons?

5. Who was the Roman goddess of the hearth, whose shrine was attended by six virgin priestesses?

6. Which winged goddess was the personification of victory in Greek mythology?

7. In Greek mythology, which golden fruit grew on a tree guarded by the Hesperides?

8. In which god's honour were the Pythian Games celebrated every four years in ancient Greece?

9. Who, in Greek mythology, was turned into the laurel which became Apollo's sacred tree?

10. Who, in Greek mythology, were the semi-divine female beings who by their songs lured men to destruction?

Music

1 Who was the 'Father of the Blues'?

2 What is a 'seguidilla'?

3 Who was the American-born harmonica player who raised the harmonica to the level of a classical instrument?

4 Who was the composer of the 'Warsaw Concerto', written for the 1942 movie 'Dangerous Moonlight'?

5 Which town in Bavaria is host to the Wagner festival?

6 Which American anthem is sung to the tune of the British National anthem 'God Save the Queen'?

7 What is meant by the musical term grazioso?

8 Who wrote the opera 'The Tales of Hoffman'?

9 What does 'sordamente' mean?

10 Who developed a unique trumpet-style of piano playing? He had an influential duet recording of 'Weather Bird' with Louis Armstrong.

General Knowledge

1 From which legendary vessel did Jesus drink at the Last Supper?

2 In which Scottish village, with the British royal family in attendance, are the main annual Highland Games held?

3 In which English cathedral was Thomas a Becket murdered?

4 The Bessemer process is used in the production of which material?

5 Las Vegas is in which U.S. state?

6 The famous tenor, John McCormack was born in which country?

7 What term applies to the producing and fitting of artificial limbs?

8 What colours are at the extreme ends of the visible light spectrum?

9 What nationality was the explorer Abel Tasman?

10 Which metal is derived from sphalerite?

Science

1   What chemical substance is formed by the interaction of an acid and a base?

2   Which alloy of tin and lead was originally used for making plates and drinking vessels?

3   What name is given to the deterioration of metal caused by repeated stresses?

4   What name is given to the speed of an object in a specified direction?

5   What name is given to a strip of paper with only one side and one edge?

6   What is the name of the milky fluid obtained from trees which is used to produce rubber?

7   The molecule of what substance contains two hydrogen atoms and one oxygen atom?

8   Which iron ore, an oxide of iron, is named in Greek after its blood-red colour?

9   In which U.S. state is the area of high-technology industries known as Silicon Valley?

10   Which green poisonous deposit forms on copper with the action of acids?

History

1. What motel chain was founded by an American hotelier, Kemmons Wilson in 1952 in Memphis, Tennessee?

2. Who was the mayor of New York from 1933-1945 who gave his name to one of that city's airports?

3. At which Ugandan city, in 1976, did a dramatic rescue of Israelis, whose plane had been hijacked by terrorists, take place?

4. Which Venetian merchant is famous for his accounts of his travels to Asia in the late 13th century?

5. Who was said to have ridden naked through the streets of Coventry in the 11th century?

6. The Colosseum in Rome is a famous example of what sort of building?

7. Which joint rulers of Spain were the parents of Joanna the Mad and patrons of Christopher Columbus?

8. After which saint is the massacre of Huguenots that began in Paris on August 24th 1572 named?

9. Which Carthaginian soldier was defeated by Scipio at Zama in 202 B.C.?

10. In ancient Rome, what name was given to the 15th day of March, May, July and October, and the 13th of other months?

Sport

1 Which institution has the motto 'citius, altius, fortuis' ('swifter, higher, stronger')?

2 Which golfer won 83 tournaments from 1935 to 1964 including the first U.S. Women's Open?

3 What was unique about the crew of the yacht 'America 3' when they won an America's Cup race in 1995?

4 The Nuggets (basketball) and Broncos (football) are major league teams of which U.S. city?

5 The name of which bird would be used for a hole in one at a par four in golf?

6 What was the nickname of Meadow Lemon who was the famed clown member of the Harlem Globetrotters basketball team?

7 In which sport might you assume the egg position?

8 The Pentathlon consists of running, riding, fencing, swimming and which other sport?

9 What sport, apart from skiing, takes place on a piste?

10 Which sports stadium in New York is affectionately known as the 'house that Babe Ruth built'?

Insects

1 Which insect is a smaller and more slender relative of the dragonfly?

_____

2 Which fly, found only in Africa, is the cause of severe anaemia and sleeping sickness?

_____

3 'Ground' and 'drywood' are two species of which insect, also known as the white ant?

_____

4 'Coleoptera' is the scientific term for which order of insects?

_____

5 Which kinds of insects have life-cycles of either 17 or 13 years?

_____

6 'Pulex irritans' is the scientific name for which common insect?

_____

7 In terms of crop destruction, which is the world's most dangerous flying insect?

_____

8 Which common pest is the fastest-flying insect known to science?

_____

9 The Devil's Coach Horse is a species of which kind of insect?

_____

10 What kind of insect is the Common wood-nymph?

General Knowledge

1 On 22nd March 2000, Bill Clinton said: 'I've wanted to come here all my life' when visiting which world-famous building?

2 In which city would you find Goulandris Natural History Museum and the Acropolis Museum?

3 In 330 A.D. which Roman emperor re-named the ancient city of Byzantium after himself?

4 What is the basic material used in origami?

5 What nationality was the famous philosopher Confucius?

6 Alaskan malamute and schnauzer are both types of what?

7 How many sides has a nonagon?

8 What does the acronym AWOL stand for?

9 Calabria, Umbria, Lombardy and Tuscany are all regions in which country?

10 Which London, England, landmark was bought by American oil tycoon Robert McCullough in 1968?

Geography

1 Which two Middle Eastern countries fought each other in a war that began in 1980?

_____

2 Of which Canadian province is Regina the capital?

_____

3 Of which Australian state is Melbourne the capital?

_____

4 Where is the chief port of the Netherlands?

_____

5 What port is at the Atlantic end of the Panama Canal?

_____

6 What might carry and deposit till and moraine?

_____

7 On which Italian river does the city of Verona stand?

_____

8 Which Sicilian port was originally called Zancle?

_____

9 In which U.S. state will you find Wichita and Topeka?

_____

10 Salt Lake City is the capital of which American state?

ROUND 29

Around the Islands

1. Which island in Brooklyn, New York, was named from the Dutch word for rabbit?

2. To which European country do the islands of Corfu and Rhodes belong?

3. On which island would you find the Arecibo radio telescope?

4. Fuerteventura, Lanzarote and Tenerife are all part of which Atlantic island group?

5. What is the name of the sea-strait between New Zealand's North Island and South Island?

6. The novel 'Captain Corelli's Mandolin' was set on which Greek island?

7. In January 2001, oil spilt from the stricken tanker 'Jessica' posed a threat to the unique wildlife on which group of islands?

8. Name the island in New York harbor which served as an entry point for immigrants to the U.S.A. between 1892 and 1943.

9. Which island country to the north-east of Madagascar has Victoria as its capital?

10. Which imaginary island was created by Sir Thomas More in 1516?

Movies

1 Which 1957 musical movie about an American movie producer in Paris who falls in love with a beautiful Russian, starred Fred Astaire and Cyd Charisse?

2 In which 1999 movie did Nicolas Cage star as a private eye on an investigation of the Hollywood porn industry?

3 Which Bernardo Bertolucci movie starred David Thewlis as a concert-pianist and Thandie Newton as his cleaner?

4 Which 1999 movie starred Robert Carlyle and Jonny Lee Miller as 18th century highwaymen and Liv Tyler as the love interest?

5 Which actor played Jan Schlictmann, a lawyer fighting for compensation for leukaemia-stricken families, in the movie 'A Civil Action'?

6 What was the name of Leslie Nielsen's character in the 'Naked Gun' movies?

7 In which 1999 movie do two teenagers get transported into the world of a black-and-white Fifties sitcom?

8 Which actor starred as advertising executive Nick Marshall in the 2000 movie 'What Women Want'?

9 Which 1987 movie starred Warren Beatty and Dustin Hoffman as untalented singer/songwriters?

10 Which 1973 movie featured Jack Nicholson as a sailor escorting a thief to naval prison?

General Knowledge

1. Chevy Chase is a suburb of which U.S. city?

2. A measure of the explosive power of an atomic weapon, what does the term 'megaton' mean?

3. 'Windflower' is an alternative name for which flower?

4. In which European city would you find the Rialto Bridge?

5. Which American actress had the nickname 'The Professional Virgin'?

6. What was the name of the 1980s trade union, formed in Gdansk, Poland and led by Lech Walesa?

7. In which country is the ski resort of Sestriere?

8. Who were the comic-book heroes 'The Dynamic Duo'?

9. Which 20th century Dutch artist is renowned for his interconnecting patterns and tricks of perspective, e.g. 'Day and Night'?

10. Which U.S. city is joined to its larger twin, Minneapolis, and is the state capital of Minnesota?

The Bible

1 In the Old Testament, which two ancient cities were destroyed by fire and brimstone?

_____

2 In the Bible, who was the father of Cain and Abel?

_____

3 In the Bible, Noah released two different species of bird to find out if there was any dry land. One was a dove, what was the other?

_____

4 The story of Noah's Ark is told in which book of the Old Testament?

_____

5 In the Old Testament, who was the elder brother of Moses?

_____

6 In the Old Testament, who was the son of Saul who formed a close friendship with David?

_____

7 In the Old Testament, who was the favourite wife of Jacob?

_____

8 Which version of the Bible was produced by St. Jerome in the 4th century A.D.?

_____

9 Which Old Testament book is the shortest in the Bible?

_____

10 According to the New Testament, which condemned robber was released at the Passover instead of Jesus?

Pop Music

1 Which group was going in 'All Directions' in their 1972 album?

_____

2 Which Irish heavy rock group claimed, in their 1978 album to be 'Live and Dangerous'?

_____

3 Which British group claimed, in their 1972 album, to be 'Fragile'?

_____

4 Whose album 'Unicorn' came out in 1970?

_____

5 The Beatles had an enormous hit with an album which they put out in 1970. What was the name of the album, taken from the lead number?

_____

6 Who wrote 'Plastic Letters' in 1977?

_____

7 Which group were 'Flogging A Dead Horse' in 1979?

_____

8 Who sang of the 'Moonflower' in 1977?

_____

9 Which British group, who were obviously fans of the Marx brothers, had an album 'A Night at the Opera' in 1975, followed by 'A Day at the Races' in 1976?

_____

10 Who had a fair-sized hit with 'Lust for Life' in 1977?

The Human Body

1. Lockjaw is another name for which medical condition?

2. What is the light-sensitive area at the back of the eye called?

3. Which basin-like structure in the body is composed of the hip bones and lower part of the spine?

4. What is the more common name for the disease varicella?

5. What sort of blood cells are also called leucocytes?

6. What name is given to a swelling in the neck caused by enlargement of the thyroid gland?

7. In the body, what are lumbar, sacral, median, ulnar, digital, maxilliary and tibial types of?

8. By what name are secretions of the lacrimal glands commonly known?

9. Which organ of the body is inflamed in a case of encephalitis?

10. Which hormone regulates the level of sugar in the blood?

Entertainment

1   Which movie star, who died in 1995, was known as the 'sweater girl'?

2   Who won best actor Oscar in 1985 for his role in 'Kiss of the Spider Woman'?

3   Immortalized in an 1897 play by Edmond Rostand, what was Cyrano de Bergerac's first name?

4   Which Irish dramatist wrote 'The Rivals' and 'The School for Scandal'?

5   The story of the Pied Piper took place in which German town?

6   Which is the highest register of male voice, which enables the singer to reach notes higher than with his natural voice?

7   How, in the world of entertainment, were LaVerne, Patty and Maxene better known in the 1940s and 1950s?

8   Who won best actress Oscar in 1990 for her role in 'Misery'?

9   Which country and western singer was known as the Silver Fox and was an originator of the countrypolitan sound?

10 Which American writer created the character Pudd'nhead Wilson in his 1894 detective story?

General Knowledge

1 In 1979, Greenland gained its independence from which country?

_____

2 What nationality was the explorer Vasco da Gama?

_____

3 In 1968, the Oscars ceremony was postponed for two days after whose assassination?

_____

4 What name is given to the region within the Arctic Circle that stretches across northern Norway, Sweden, Finland and into the Kola peninsula of Russia?

_____

5 What is the common name of the wasp Vespa crabro?

_____

6 Algeria and Tunisia both gained independence from which European country?

_____

7 In physics, what N is the central core of the atom?

_____

8 What is the middle colour of the spectrum?

_____

9 According to sailor's folklore, what is the name of the ghost ship that is supposed to haunt the seas around the Cape of Good Hope? The story inspired an opera by Wagner.

_____

10 In which country is the ski resort of Cavalese, where 20 people were killed when an American military aircraft sliced through the steel wire supporting a cable car in 1998?

History

1 What was the name of the pupil that theologian and philosopher Peter Abelard married in secret?

2 Which Egyptian diplomat was the secretary-general of the United Nations from 1992 to 1996?

3 Which Frankish ruler was the grandfather of Charlemagne?

4 What became the official instrument of execution in France during the French Revolution?

5 In which American city was John F. Kennedy assassinated in 1963?

6 Which European country ruled the African country of Zaire prior to its independence?

7 Which French noblewoman assassinated Jean-Paul Marat in his bath?

8 Which former coal mining village in South Wales was the scene of a 1966 disaster that killed 116 children?

9 Which modern city was known as Byzantium from 660 B.C. to 330 A.D.?

10 Which ancient calculating device consists of a frame of wires on which beads are strung?

'The Simpsons'

1 Bart's arch-enemy, real name Robert Underdunk Terwilliger, is better known by which name?

_____

2 What was the name of the store that Ned Flanders opened in Springfield Mall, offering tools and gadgets for left handed-only people?

_____

3 What type of transportation system was introduced to Springfield after salesman, Lyle Lanley pointed out that the town of North Haverbrook invested in it and had thrived as a result?

_____

4 What was the name of Ned Flanders' wife?

_____

5 What are the names of Marge Simpson's two sisters?

_____

6 What is the name of the comic-book store owned by the sneering, overweight Comic Book Guy?

_____

7 Who is nuclear power plant owner Montgomery Burns' fawning assistant?

_____

8 Who is the idiot son of idiot police chief Clancy Wiggum?

_____

9 Who is the grey-haired anchorman Channel 6 news reader?

_____

10 According to the spooky song in 'The Simpsons' movie, what does the Spider-Pig do?

Literature

1. Who wrote 'The History of the Decline and Fall of the Roman Empire'?

2. Which American author wrote 'Charlotte's Web' and 'Stuart Little'?

3. What was the pen name of the novelist and literary critic Cicely Isabel Fairfield?

4. What C is an 18th century Italian writer of erotic memoirs?

5. Which American humorist's pieces are contained in 'Crazy Like a Fox' and 'Baby, It's Cold Inside'?

6. What was the real name of the novelist who used the pen name George Eliot?

7. Which Irish dramatist wrote 'The Playboy of the Western World'?

8. Which Austrian-born philosopher wrote 'Philosophical Investigations'?

9. Who wrote 'The Three Musketeers'?

10. What was the pen name of American short-story writer William Sidney Porter?

General Knowledge

1. The staple diet of the silkworm are the leaves of which bush?

2. Which actor's dour expression earned him the nickname of 'The Great Stoneface'?

3. What were the first names of the pioneering aviators, the Wright brothers?

4. How many pints are in fifteen gallons?

5. What was the name of Hiawatha's wife?

6. 'Somewhere' and 'America' are songs in which musical?

7. The Greek island of Corfu lies close to the coast of which former communist country?

8. In which Italian city is the Uffizi art museum and the Piazza della Signoria?

9. Which German-born artist was court painter to Henry VIII of England?

10. What is the capital of the Greek island of Crete?

Numbers

1 How many were the 'Labours of Hercules'?

_____

2 How many are the 'Pillars of Islam', the primary requirements of that religion?

_____

3 How many are the Muses of Greek mythology?

_____

4 What is the number of Mozart's last symphony, nicknamed 'The Jupiter'?

_____

5 What are the first four prime numbers?

_____

6 Which number of the 'Apollo' space mission series first took astronauts to the Moon?

_____

7 Aglaia, Euphroysne and Thalia, of Greek mythology are collectively known as what?

_____

8 Faith and Hope are the first two of the three virtues; what is the third?

_____

9 Sanguine, Melancholic, Choleric and Lethargic were thought to be the basic personality types collectively known as the Four what?

_____

10 The Book of Numbers is the fourth book of the Bible of which religion?

War

1 Which war lasted from 1936-1939?

2 In which war were the Battles of Bull Run fought?

3 Ultra was the British code name for which German cipher machine?

4 'Oswiecim' is the Polish name for which notorious German World War II extermination and concentration camp?

5 Which large plain in Argentina, Paraguay and Bolivia was the cause of a war in the 1930s?

6 In what year was the Spanish-American War?

7 Who was the official propagandist of Nazi Germany?

8 What is Willy Messerschmitt famous for designing?

9 Who was the commander-in-chief of the Greeks in the Trojan War who was murdered by his wife Clytemnestra?

10 In which U.S. state is Los Alamos, where the first atom bombs were made?

Comedy

1. Which comedy duo starred in the movies 'Sons of the Desert', 'Babes in Toyland', 'Saps at Sea', and 'Way Out West', to name but a few?

2. One of the Marx Brothers, what was the nickname of the comedian, actor, singer and writer born Julius Henry in October 1890?

3. Which English actor played The Little Tramp in 'The Circus', 'City Lights', and 'The Kid'?

4. Who directed the movies 'Some Like It Hot', 'The Seven-Year Itch', and 'The Apartment'?

5. Born Nathan Birnbaum, which American comedian was popular for more than 70 years in vaudeville, radio, film, and television?

6. Which American comedian was born in Virginia, grew up in Mecklenburg County, North Carolina and is part Cherokee?

7. Who created TV's 'The Simpsons' and 'Futurama'?

8. Who sang the novelty song 'Hello Mother, Hello Father (A Letter from Camp)'?

9. 'Robin Hood: Men in Tights' was produced and directed by whom?

10. Born Jerome Silberman in Milwaukee, Wisconsin on 11 June 1933, by what name is the comedy actor, director and screenwriter better known?

Sport

1 What is the name of the world's longest official downhill ski-run at Mürren in Switzerland?

2 Which Austrian former Formula One driver also founded two airlines?

3 Who was the first black woman to win the (tennis) U.S. Open, in 1957?

4 In golf, an 'albatross' is how many strokes under or over par?

5 What was the nickname of Englishman, Michael Edwards, the amateur ski-jumper who came last at the 1988 Winter Olympics?

6 Athlete, Jesse Owens is said to have had his 'finest hour' at which Olympics?

7 Excluding Antarctica, which continent is the only one never to have hosted the Olympic Games?

8 Wilt Chamberlain holds the record for scoring 100 points in a single game, in which sport?

9 Which national team won the first Fifa World Cup title in 1930?

10 Which boxer is the only one to win the World Heavyweight title three times; in 1964, '74 and '78?

General Knowledge

1 In which Canadian province is the country's capital, Ottawa, situated?

2 What is the name of the Russian who gave his name to the famous AK47 assault rifle?

3 Which two primary colours are mixed to make purple?

4 What is the name of the sedative drug which caused deformities in babies born in the late 1950s and early 1960s?

5 Tarabulus is the Arabic name for two cities. One is the capital of an African country, the other a port in Lebanon. By what name do we know these cities?

6 Writer P.L. Travers created the character Mary Poppins. What do the initials P.L. stand for?

7 A hexagon is a polygon with how many sides?

8 In which country did the dance, the gavotte, originate?

9 In Roman numerals, what number is represented by L?

10 In the 1950s, which company marketed the first Japanese transistor radio?

Classical Music

1 What does 'francamente' mean?

2 What does 'calando' mean?

3 What is the name of the Oratorio for solo voices, choir and orchestra, Opus 70 composed by Felix Mendelssohn?

4 Sir Edward Elgar's 'Enigma Variations' are 14 variations on an original theme. What does each variation represent?

5 'The Great Gate of Kiev' is the final section of which composition by Mussorgsky?

6 Who composed the orchestral rhapsody 'Espana'?

7 Who composed the 'Music for the Royal Fireworks'?

8 Ottorino Respighi composed three orchestral suites inspired by his favourite city - Rome. One was ' The Fountains of Rome'; another was 'The Pines of Rome'. What was the third?

9 'Bolero' is one of the most popular works of which French composer?

10 Name the 20th century Italian-born American composer who wrote the operas 'Amelia Goes To The Ball' and 'Amahl And The Night Visitors'.

Science

1. What name is given to a semiconductor device with three or more electrodes?

_____

2. Of what is the sensitivity or speed usually quoted as an ISO rating?

_____

3. What name is given to the branch of zoology that involves the study of birds?

_____

4. What name is given to the branch of biology involving the study of fungi?

_____

5. What nationality was the Nobel prize winning nuclear physicist Niels Bohr?

_____

6. Cr is the chemical symbol for what?

_____

7. Which category in the biological classification of animals can be divided into classes?

_____

8. What name is given to the process by which green plants exposed to sunlight produce carbohydrates?

_____

9. The Periodic Table is a list of chemical elements. What is No. 1 in that list?

_____

10. Pb is the chemical symbol for what?

Geography

1 Through which three European countries do the Ardennes hills extend?

___

2 Of which South American country is Asunción the capital?

___

3 In the U.S.A., what is the largest of the New England states?

___

4 On which major river is the Aswan High Dam situated?

___

5 How are the Canadian provinces of Alberta, Manitoba, and Saskatchewan collectively known?

___

6 Which is the second largest country in the world?

___

7 Which present-day country contains the ancient country of Parthia?

___

8 In which country is the Grande Dixence Dam?

___

9 Which country is also known as the Republic of China?

___

10 Of which ocean is the Caribbean Sea a section?

General Knowledge

1 Which famous bandleader disappeared on a flight from England to France in December 1944?

2 The Kamchatka peninsula in the Pacific Ocean belongs to which country?

3 Lego bricks originated in which European country?

4 Which Russian-born, American songwriter's original name was Israel Baline?

5 Robert Baden-Powell founded which organization in 1907?

6 Which archipelago is sited at the southern tip of South America?

7 The Royal house of which country is called the House of Orange?

8 The Saanen is a breed of which farm animal?

9 Which series of passenger aircraft, built by Boeing, is the best-selling type in aviation history?

10 Which colony was ceded back to China by Portugal in 1999?

History

1 Which household appliance was patented by Percy Spencer, an American working for Raytheon, in the 1940s?

2 Which famous German automatic pistol was named after the man who first developed it in 1902?

3 In which Italian city was the explorer Marco Polo born?

4 What was the popular name for the East German secret police who were disbanded shortly after the Berlin Wall came down in 1989?

5 Which famous park was officially opened in New York in 1876?

6 Said to have lived in a tub, who founded the philosophical sect known as the Cynics?

7 What was the surname of Julius and Ethel, the married couple found guilty of spying and executed at Sing Sing prison in 1953?

8 What name was given to the ceremonial distribution of gifts practised by native American people of the N.W. Pacific coast region?

9 Which 'King of the Wild Frontier' was born in Greene County, Tennessee on 17 August 1786?

10 In the 16th century, the prophecies of which man were collected together in the work entitled 'Centuries'?

Movies

1 Which actor was Oscar-nominated in 1999 for his role as Bill Paxton's older brother in the movie 'A Simple Plan'?

_____

2 In which Pygmalion-esque 1999 movie did a high school sports hero transform a nerd into a prom queen?

_____

3 In which 1968 movie did Julie Christie and Richard Chamberlain play an unhappily-married couple?

_____

4 In which 2000 movie did Nicolas Cage star as a wealthy stockbroker who finds himself in a parallel life?

_____

5 Which 1974 movie directed by, and starring, Sidney Poitier, also featured Bill Cosby and Richard Pryor?

_____

6 Which 2000 movie by M. Night Shyamalan starred Bruce Willis as a security guard who escapes a fatal train derailment?

_____

7 Who won a Best Actor Oscar for his performance in the 1967 movie 'In the Heat of the Night'?

_____

8 Which 1973 movie starred Barbra Streisand and Robert Redford as lovers who meet on a college campus of the late 1930s?

_____

9 Which 1987 movie starred Anne Bancroft as New York writer Helene Hanff and Anthony Hopkins as Frank Doel, an antiquarian bookseller in London?

_____

10 Which 1991 movie featured a family of giant beetles disguised as humans in order to save the Brazilian rain forest?

Food and Drink

1. Which fruit is a cross between a grapefruit and a tangerine?

2. Which flavouring is the root-like stem of the tropical plant, Zingibar officinale?

3. What is the common name of Allium cepa, a biennial plant of the lily family native to South West Asia?

4. Derived from the Latin for 'Greek hay', what F is a herb of the pea family whose aromatic seeds are used as a spice?

5. Known to the French as persil, which herb with curled aromatic leaves is used in cooking?

6. Dark Muscovado and Light Muscovado are both types of what?

7. What is the chief protein in milk and cheese?

8. What is the main ingredient of the Swiss food dish, rosti?

9. The name of which type of pasta is derived from the Italian for 'little cords'?

10. What do the initials of the meat substitute TVP stand for?

Distinguished Duos

1. Which opera by Leoncavallo is sometimes featured in a double-bill with Mascagni's 'Cavalleria Rusticana', the pair having the nickname 'Cav and Pag'?

2. Which British comedy-duo's Christmas 1971 TV 'special' went down in history due to a spoof performance of Grieg's piano concerto, conducted by a bewildered Andre Previn?

3. Which 1970s American cop-duo TV series, was made into a 2004 film starring Ben Stiller and Owen Wilson?

4. What nationality were the famous singing-duo, Nina and Frederik?

5. How are singing-duo, Bobby Hatfield and Bill Medley, better known?

6. Who were the 'star-crossed lovers', offspring of the Montague and Capulet families?

7. Which folk-rock duo originally called themselves 'Tom and Jerry'?

8. Which fairy tale children were abandoned in the forest when their parents were no longer able to feed them?

9. Which cartoon couple reside at 62 West Wallaby Street, Wigan, England?

10. In Shakespeare's 'Hamlet', who are the two court stewards that the king sends to spy on Hamlet?

General Knowledge

1 Shogi is a Japanese form of which board game?

2 In which country was the feminist and author Germaine Greer born?

3 Which ageing 'playboy' married Kimberley Conrad in 1989?

4 By what name was the Colt 45 revolver popularly known?

5 What sort of gemstone is the jewel known as the Star of India?

6 Which sign of the zodiac is known as 'The Scales'?

7 Which of the seven deadly sins begins with the letter C?

8 What colour is traditionally associated with envy or jealousy?

9 16th century Spaniards believed there was a region of South America made entirely of gold. What name did they give it?

10 From which country does Capodimonte porcelain come?

Language

1. What is the name for a word or phrase that reads the same both forwards and backwards, such as 'level', or 'Dennis and Edna sinned'?

2. What is the literal meaning of the Russian word 'Kremlin'?

3. Which profession gets its name from the Latin word for the soft metal, lead?

4. In Britain it is a nappy, what is it called in North America?

5. What predominantly Irish Christian name means 'small dark one'?

6. What is the English name for what the French call La Manche?

7. What O is a figure of speech such as 'cruel to be kind'?

8. Which language is an official language of Canada, Belgium and Switzerland?

9. Which expression, meaning in a meaningless or complicated language, is derived from the name of an African tribal god Mama Dyumbo?

10. Which French phrase describes an alluring or seductive woman, especially one who causes men to love her to their own distress?

Poetry

1 Which Irish poet won the 1995 Nobel Prize for Literature?

2 According to Longfellow, which Indian was married to Minnehaha?

3 Which Scottish poet wrote 'To a Mouse' and 'To a Louse'?

4 To which British poet was Sylvia Plath married?

5 Who wrote 'Portrait of the Artist as a Young Dog'?

6 Which English poet wrote 'L'Allegro' and 'Il Penseroso'?

7 Which Roman poet, exiled under the emperor Domitian, is best known for his 16 Satires?

8 Which U.S. poet and short-story writer wrote 'The Raven'?

9 Which British metaphysical poet wrote the religious works collected in 'The Temple'?

10 Name the American poet who made broadcasts in Italy supporting the Fascists during the Second World War.

Religion

1   In which country is the Coptic Church sect?

2   Which Christian festival occurs on the 6th of January?

3   On which date is All Saints' Day?

4   Who is the patron saint of children?

5   Which third-fourth century ruler became the first Christian Roman emperor?

6   By whom was the Unification Church founded in 1954?

7   In which country was the Unification Church founded?

8   In which present-day country was the Zoroastrian religion founded around 750 B.C.?

9   William Miller founded which church movement in the 19th century?

10   Which French king was declared a saint in 1297?

General Knowledge

1. The psychic performer Uri Geller was born in which country?

2. CO is the chemical formula for what?

3. Caracas is the capital of which South American country?

4. Which world leader was given the nickname 'The Beard' by the United States Intelligence Service?

5. What do birds do when they nidificate?

6. Described as the 'greatest mind and paramount icon of our age', who did Time magazine name as their 'Person of the 20th Century'?

7. What type of creature is an addax?

8. What sort of projectiles were pioneered by American physicist Robert Hutchings Goddard?

9. Which Asian plant yields marijuana and a tough fibre used for rope?

10. In architecture, fenestration is the arrangement of what in a building?

ROUND 59

Music

1 Which Beatle was the group's rhythm guitarist?

_____

2 The musical instrument, the ocarina, is made of what material?

_____

3 Which instrument is played by blues artist B.B. King?

_____

4 What was the nickname of country-blues folk singer Huddie Leadbetter?

_____

5 In the U.S., which Nat King Cole recording was the first song, in 1948, to enter radio's 'The Hit Parade' at the No. 1 position?

_____

6 Which Canadian soloist brought out the album 'Mirror Ball' in 1995?

_____

7 The Bee Gees brought out a very reassuring album in 1993. What was its title?

_____

8 Who issued her 'Birthday Concert' album in 1997?

_____

9 Which group rang 'The Division Bell' in 1994?

_____

10 Which group led us into 'Hell's Ditch' in 1990?

Nature

1 Which astronomical phenomena are also called shooting stars or falling stars?

2 What name is given to a butterfly or moth in its larval stage?

3 What substance do bees collect from flowers and turn into honey?

4 Which order of mammals includes kangaroos and wallabies?

5 Which land bird has the largest wing span?

6 Which fish related to the carp has the scientific name Tinca tinca?

7 What name is given to a creature that lacks a backbone?

8 What name is given to the poisonous substance produced by snakes and scorpions?

9 What are a cat's vibrissae more commonly known as?

10 Which seabird is also known as bottlenose or sea parrot?

Mythology

1. Who was the Roman goddess of flowers?

2. What is the name of the ancient temple on the Acropolis in Athens that was dedicated to the goddess Athena?

3. In Greek mythology, who fell in love with Psyche?

4. In Greek mythology, who was the messenger and herald of the gods?

5. According to Greek mythology, how many Fates were there?

6. According to Greek mythology, how many Muses were there?

7. According to Arthurian legend, what was the capital of King Arthur's kingdom?

8. According to Greek mythology, by what name were the 12 children of Uranus and Gaea collectively known?

9. Which mischievous elf in Irish folklore is supposed to have a hidden store of gold?

10. In Arthurian legend, who was King Arthur's enchantress sister?

History

1 Seven kings of which country have been named Haakon?

2 Which method of execution was abolished by the Roman emperor, Constantine?

3 Which English naval administrator is chiefly remembered for his diary which gives an account of the Great Fire of London?

4 Which Prussian general who fought at Waterloo was known as Marshal Forward?

5 In what did Cleopatra supposedly bathe to remain beautiful?

6 Whose tomb was discovered by Howard Carter and Lord Carnarvon in Egypt in 1922?

7 Which infamous person was born the son of a customs official in Braunau, upper Austria in 1889?

8 How did American financier John Jacob Astor IV die in 1912?

9 Which famous Paris landmark was constructed between 1806 and 1836 to celebrate the victories of Napoleon?

10 What type of ancient creature was found preserved in the frozen wastes of Siberia in 1999?

General Knowledge

1 Which French king was guillotined in the French Revolution?

2 By what name was Gaius Caesar Augustus Germanicus better known?

3 In what type of business did the Greek multi-millionaire Aristotle Onassis make his fortune?

4 What, in Internet terminology, does FTP stand for?

5 In computer terminology, what does the acronym ROM stand for?

6 Which religion, that originated in ancient Persia, was centred upon the worship of the God of Light and Truth?

7 Who, in 1993, became America's first woman Attorney General?

8 Who played the part of the heroine in the original movie 'King Kong', released in 1933?

9 What, in Internet terminology, does LAN stand for?

10 The Ligurian Sea is an arm of which body of water?

Sport

1 In the Central Asian region horseback sport of buzkashi, what is traditionally fought over by the two teams?

2 What kind of race is the Vasaloppet, held each year in central Sweden?

3 The Curtis Cup is awarded is awarded to women players of which sport?

4 In 2009, who achieved a world record time of 9.58 seconds in the 100 metres sprint?

5 What nationality is Formula One former driver Keke Rosberg?

6 In which years of the 20th century were the Olympic Games cancelled due to war?

7 What was the name of the 1981 Epsom Derby-winning racehorse, kidnapped in 1983 and never seen since?

8 The Thrilla in Manila was the name given to a 1975 boxing match between which two heavyweights?

9 Which country's Formula One circuit is sited at Estoril?

10 Which English football team's players were involved in the 1958 air-crash at Munich?

Literature

1 Which novel by Charles Dickens features Bill Sikes and Fagin?

_____

2 Who wrote 'Other Voices, Other Rooms' and 'In Cold Blood'?

_____

3 Which Scottish historian and essayist wrote 'The French Revolution'?

_____

4 Which New Zealand-born short-story writer wrote 'Bliss' and 'The Garden Party'?

_____

5 Which late eighteenth century literary movement's name means 'storm and stress' in German?

_____

6 Which American novelist wrote 'The Red Badge of Courage'?

_____

7 Which Italian novelist wrote 'The Woman of Rome' and 'Two Women'?

_____

8 Which author created the British intelligence officer George Smiley?

_____

9 Which American novelist wrote 'Goodbye, Columbus' and 'Portnoy's Complaint'?

_____

10 Which U.S. author wrote 'Another Country' and 'The Fire Next Time'?

Space

1. Which is the brightest star in the constellation Virgo?

2. In which decade of the 20th century was Halley's Comet last seen?

3. Which star constellation is known as the 'water bearer'?

4. In which constellation is the red giant Aldebaran?

5. U.S. space shuttles are officially referred to by the initials STS. What does STS stand for?

6. Phobos and Deimos are satellites of which planet?

7. To the nearest whole number, what percentage of the mass of the solar system resides in the Sun?

8. Which constellation is popularly known as the Southern Cross?

9. In 1962, who became the first American to orbit the Earth?

10. Sent into orbit by the Russians, what was the name of the Samoyed who was the first dog in space?

General Knowledge

1 Which singer topped the singles charts in 1973 with 'Can the Can'?

2 Cape Horn is the southernmost tip of which continent?

3 What kind of animal was Beatrice Potter character, Mrs Tiggy-Winkle?

4 'Two-Faced Woman' was the last film of which Swedish actress?

5 Which holy city was captured by Saladin in 1187?

6 Which London park adjoins Kensington Gardens?

7 Which birthstone applies to a person born in April?

8 The Mindanao Trench is located in which ocean?

9 Benazir Bhutto was the first female leader of which country?

10 The Brenner Pass is a road and rail pass that connects which two countries?

Rivers and Mountains

1   Kicking Horse Pass is a pass through which range of mountains?

2   In which country does the River Rhine rise?

3   Of which country is Mount Logan the highest mountain?

4   The Ancient Greek town of Delphi, famous for the Temple of Apollo, was on the south slope of which mountain?

5   Which French city on the River Deule is the capital of the Nord department?

6   Annapurna is a mountain in which range?

7   Which European river is crossed by the Vasco da Gama bridge?

8   Between which two countries does the Cascade Range of volcanic mountains extend?

9   What river in Florence, Italy, is crossed by the Ponte Vecchio?

10 Which river rises in the Rocky Mountains and forms the border between Texas and Mexico?

Politics

1 In May 1999 who succeeded Benjamin Netanyahu as Israel's Prime Minister?

2 Jomo Kenyatta was prime minister and president of which African country?

3 Who was the Democrat candidate beaten by George Bush in the 1988 U.S. presidential election?

4 Who was the president of the Confederate States during the American Civil War?

5 After her husband had been assassinated in 1983, who became president of the Philippines in 1986?

6 After which U.S. politician was the Prohibition Act of 1919 named?

7 Who was U.S. president when the armistice ending the Korean War was signed on 27 July 1953?

8 Which Italian statesman, writer and political philosopher wrote 'The Prince'?

9 Nelson Rockefeller was governor of which U.S. state during the 1950s and 1960s?

10 16 October 1995 saw the largest gathering of black people in Washington since Martin Luther King made his famous "I have a dream" speech in 1963. What name was given to that gathering?

Geography

1. In which American state is the town of Tombstone, famous in Westerns?

2. Which is the second largest city in the Republic of Ireland?

3. Which is the largest city in China?

4. Which Asian country changed its name to Myanmar in 1989?

5. In which sea-strait, situated between Sicily and the Italian mainland, is the mirage known as Fata Morgana occasionally seen?

6. Of which European country is Krakow the third largest city?

7. In which U.S. state is the city of Milwaukee?

8. Which large bay, an inlet of the Atlantic Ocean between northern Spain and western France, is noted for its rough seas and high tides?

9. Which former capital of Japan is an anagram of its present capital?

10. Which archipelago, divided between Chile and Argentina, is separated from the South American mainland by the Strait of Magellan?

Movies

1 Which 1999 movie by Neil LaBute starred Jason Patric, Ben Stiller and Nastassja Kinski?

2 Which 1952 movie starring Robert Mitchum and Jane Russell was set in a Portuguese colony south of Hong Kong?

3 Which 1978 thriller starred Faye Dunaway as a fashion photographer and Tommy Lee Jones as a police lieutenant?

4 Which 1991 movie starred John Malkovich and Andie MacDowell as a couple holed up in a London hotel?

5 Which actor played commander of King Company Lt. Joe Clemons in the 1959 movie set during the Korean War, 'Pork Chop Hill'?

6 Which 1985 movie starred John Travolta and Jamie Lee Curtis as a journalist and an aerobics instructor respectively?

7 Which actor played Death in the movie 'Meet Joe Black', a remake of 1934's 'Death Takes a Holiday'?

8 Which actress played the oppressive mother of Adam Sandler's college football hero in the 1999 movie 'The Waterboy'?

9 Which actress played Odessa the maid to Sissy Spacek's upper-middle-class housewife in the 1990 movie 'The Long Walk Home'?

10 In which 1988 movie did Sean Penn and Robert Duvall star as Danny McGavin and Bob Hodges, members of the gang crime division of the LAPD?

General Knowledge

1 What in Buddhism is the attainment of supreme bliss?

2 The River Danube flows into which sea?

3 Which is the smallest woodwind instrument?

4 Which is the largest woodwind instrument?

5 Which country is sandwiched between Austria to the West and Romania to the East?

6 Which religion celebrates Navarati, or The Festival of Nine Nights?

7 What in the U.S.A. is the Palmetto state?

8 Who was the star of the 1928 movie 'Steamboat Willie'?

9 Who wrote the opera 'Cavallaria Rusticana'?

10 What is a gingko a type of?

Pop Music

1 Which group had an album entitled 'Heartbeat City' in 1984?

_____

2 Which group was 'Dressed to Kill' in 1975?

_____

3 Which group had a hit in 1965 with 'Rubber Soul'?

_____

4 Which group cut an album in 1962 called 'Green Onions'?

_____

5 The American group The Byrds had two hit albums in 1966. One was 'Turn, Turn, Turn'. What was the other?

_____

6 Who was the British soloist who had a hit with 'The Universal Soldier' in 1966?

_____

7 In 1967, The Doors put out two major albums. One was called 'The Doors'. What was the other?

_____

8 Which pop icon issued an album in 1968 in honour of 'John Wesley Harding'?

_____

9 Who put out the album 'Can't Get Enough' in 1974 as a launch-pad for the number 'Can't Get Enough of Your Love Babe'?

_____

10 Who had a hit with 'Fear of Music' in 1979?

History

1   What nationality was the prince who lived from 1394 until 1460 and known as Henry the Navigator?

2   Which American married couple were executed for spying in 1953?

3   Which 17th century French mathematician was famous for his last theorem?

4   Which movie star's death at the age of 31 in August 1926 reportedly led to worldwide hysteria and several suicides?

5   Which prison was demolished after the death of its last inmate, Rudolf Hess?

6   Whom did Jacqueline Kennedy, widow of John F. Kennedy, marry in 1968?

7   Which Asian capital city was known as Batavia until 1949?

8   Who was emperor of Rome at the time of the fire that destroyed much of the city in 64 A.D.?

9   Of which revolution was the Reign of Terror a feature?

10 Which famous American sharpshooter was the subject of the musical 'Annie Get Your Gun'?

The Animal Kingdom

1 Snake-necked and Hawksbill are what kinds of creature?

2 What would you find in a vespiary?

3 What bird of prey is also known as fish hawk or fish eagle?

4 Which small parrots get their name from the great affection they show to their mates?

5 Which highly venomous snake has 'king' and 'spitting' varieties?

6 Which hoofed African mammal of the giraffe family was unknown to Europeans until 1901?

7 What creature is a caiman a type of?

8 A whooper is a type of which bird?

9 What name is given to the process of exterminating pests using smoke or gases?

10 Which fish gets its name from its long whisker-like barbels?

General Knowledge

1. On a watch-face, how many degrees of a circle lie between 14.00 hours and 20.00 hours?

2. Colonel Gadaffi, John F Kennedy and Mick Jagger all attended which London university?

3. Which country in particular celebrates the annual Day of the Dead?

4. Baba Yaga, a witch who lives in a hut which moves around on chicken's legs, is a figure from the folklore of which particular country?

5. Who was the god of the north wind in Greek mythology?

6. Which Beatles' single was the first to reach No. 1 in both the U.K. and the U.S.?

7. Kastrup airport serves which European capital city?

8. Multiply by nine, divide by five, add 32 is the formula for which conversion?

9. Which kind of cinema opened on 6th June 1933, in Pennsauken, New Jersey?

10. The 'Tin Lizzie' was a nickname for which early car?

Entertainment

1. Emperor Ming the Merciless was the arch-enemy of which sci-fi hero?

2. How in the world of rock 'n' roll music is Richard Penniman better known?

3. Which place in Georgia, U.S.A., the birthplace of Kim Basinger and where the members of the group REM spent their formative years, is also the name of a European capital city?

4. Which 1973 Woody Allen movie was set in the year 2173?

5. Which American singer, famous for his relaxed style, died on 12 May 2001, just days short of his 89th birthday?

6. The singers Neil Young, Joni Mitchell and Alanis Morissette were all born in which country?

7. What famous announcement was made by concert hosts to signify to fans that an Elvis Presley concert was over?

8. In which German city is the famous 'Oktoberfest' beer festival held?

9. What was the Academy Award winning song in the 1940 Disney movie 'Pinocchio'?

10. If Batman is Bruce Wayne and Robin is Dick Grayson, who is Batwoman?

Ballets

1 'Les Syphides' is a ballet performed to the music of which composer?

2 Which American composed the scores for 'Billy the Kid' and 'Rodeo'?

3 The famous 'Ritual Fire Dance' is part of which ballet by Manuel de Falla?

4 'Swan Lake' and 'The Sleeping Beauty' are two of the 'big three' ballets by Tchaikovsky; what is the third?

5 Which ballet by Stravinsky caused a riot at its first performance in Paris, in 1913?

6 In which ballet by Delibes does a real girl fool a toymaker into thinking she is one of his creations?

7 The scores for the ballets 'Spartacus' and 'Gayaneh' were composed by which 20th century Armenian composer?

8 Which Russian composed music for 'Petrushka' and 'The Firebird'?

9 What nationality was Alberto Ginastera, composer of ballet music on South American themes, e.g. 'Estancia'?

10 Which 1935 ballet by Prokofiev was based on a play by William Shakespeare?

Computing

1   What do the initials C.A.D. stand for?

2   Originally called the Memory Disk, the Floppy Disk was invented by which company?

3   Which major computer company started out in a garage in Palo Alto, California in 1939?

4   The resolution of digital cameras is stated in which units?

5   Introduced in 1946- 47, what was the first electronic computer?

6   Which company is the main producer of the Pentium microprocessor?

7   Computer-generated 3D graphics were first used, exclusively, in which film of 1995?

8   What do the initials R.A.M. stand for?

9   The main circuit board in a P.C. is commonly known by what name?

10 Microsoft's Windows 1.0 was launched in which year?

Travel and Transport

1. Which Russian port on the Pacific Ocean rim is the eastern terminus of the Trans-Siberian railway?

2. Which American city is served by Hartsfield International airport?

3. Who is the patron saint of travellers?

4. Which famous World War II fighter plane was designed by Reginald Mitchell?

5. On which vessel did Charles Darwin make his voyage of discovery?

6. The Orient Express first ran between Europe and which Middle East country?

7. Who invented the first helicopter?

8. Launched by the U.S. in 1954, what was the name of the first nuclear submarine?

9. What Ford vehicle letter, in 1927, denoted the car that succeeded the model T?

10. What was the 'Tin Donkey', which in 1915 was the first of its kind?

ROUND 81

General Knowledge

1. Which Italian fashion designer was murdered outside his Miami home in July 1997?

2. Pope Gregory VIII introduced which calendar, in 1582?

3. What is the most abundant gas in our atmosphere?

4. Which present-day country did the Romans call Hibernia?

5. With 190 member states, which police organization is based in Lyon, France?

6. In which Shakespeare play do rivals Mercutio and Tybalt appear?

7. Which of Disney's 'seven dwarfs' didn't have a beard?

8. Who was the founder of the State of Israel?

9. With which planet did the comet, Shoemaker-Levy 9, collide in 1994?

10. In 54 A.D., who poisoned the Roman emperor Claudius, so that her son Nero could accede to the title?

Sport and Games

1. What is the name of the flat circular disc of vulcanized rubber used in the game of ice-hockey?

2. In chess, which piece can move diagonally in a straight line but keeping to the colour of the square on which it starts?

3. Which American former tennis champion was born in Wiesbaden, Germany on 16 February, 1959?

4. What was invented in 1839 by a West Point cadet, Abner Doubleday?

5. In which country is the Imola motor racing circuit?

6. How many players are there in a volleyball team?

7. In which country did ice hockey originate?

8. Which former tennis player (he won the Australian Open in 1977 and was a regular around New York's nightlife) was found dead in September 1994?

9. Name the Italian city which stages horse races through the main square during the annual Palio festival.

10. Which Russian became the youngest ever world chess champion at the age of 22 in 1985?

The Bible

1 Which are the only two angels named in the Bible?

_____

2 Which battle is said by the Bible to occur at the end of the world?

_____

3 The Decalogue is an alternative name for what?

_____

4 The Tower of Babel is mentioned in which book of the Bible?

_____

5 The portentous 'writing on the wall' mentioned in the Book of Daniel, appears to which Babylonian king?

_____

6 How old was Methuselah when he died?

_____

7 Of which kind of wood did God instruct Noah to build the Ark?

_____

8 Which trio were cast into the 'fiery furnace'?

_____

9 What miracle did Jesus perform at the wedding at Cana?

_____

10 What is the collective name of the first five books of the Old Testament?

Science

1 Of which science are quantum mechanics and thermodynamics branches?

2 What name is given to the opposition in an electrical circuit to the flow of an alternating current, which has the symbol Z?

3 Of what are the Perseids, Leonids and Geminids examples?

4 What name is given to precipitation containing high levels of sulphuric and nitric acids?

5 Which alloy was first mass-produced by using the Bessemer process?

6 Which branch of mathematics takes its name from the Greek for 'Earth measurement'?

7 Used with reference to the explosive power of a nuclear weapon, what word is used to describe the equivalent explosive force of one million tons of TNT?

8 What is the smallest unit of a compound that can exist independently and retain its properties?

9 What is the more common name of trichloromethane?

10 In which decade of the 20th century was insulin first used to treat diabetes?

General Knowledge

1. What is the Latin motto on the Great Seal of the United States of America?

2. The parietal bone is in which part of the human body?

3. What is the meaning of the commonly-used Arabic word 'Inshallah'?

4. Which actor's daughter Cheyenne committed suicide in Tahiti in 1995?

5. In South America, the rivers Uruguay and Parana combine above Buenos Aires to form which river?

6. What nationality was the explorer Robert Peary?

7. The Puerto Rico Trench is the deepest point of which ocean?

8. Which was the first great Roman road which linked Rome with present day Brindisi?

9. What is the traditional Chinese practice of inserting needles into selected points in the body called?

10. Which hypothetical substance did alchemists seek for its ability to turn base metals into gold?

History

1 On what date in July do the French celebrate Bastille Day?

2 Who was the wife of the Emperor Augustus and mother of the Emperor Tiberius?

3 What name was given to the followers of the Greek moral philosopher Diogenes of Sinope?

4 Which Greek philosopher founded the Academy in Athens in about 387 B.C.?

5 Mazzini and Garibaldi did much to unite which country?

6 Born in 1811, Chang and Eng were the world's first officially recorded what?

7 What name was given to the government of Germany from 1919 to 1933, named after the town in which the constitution was formulated?

8 What was the name of German terrorist Andreas Baader's female partner?

9 What was the name of the urban guerrilla organization headed by Baader and his partner?

10 Which British conductor was music director of the New York Philharmonic from 1937 to 1942 and thereafter principal conductor of the Hallé Orchestra in Manchester, until his death in 1970?

Jazz

1 Which famous jazz trumpeter was given the nickname 'Little Jazz'?

2 Who was the Toledo, Ohio born pianist who, although near blind since birth, was the most influential 'swing' style pianist in his day?

3 Who do you think of when you hear 'Take Five' or 'Unsquare Dance'?

4 Which Danish-born trombonist, who played with many of the jazz greats, was co-founder with J.J. Johnson of their own jazz quintet?

5 Who was the Belgian-born, self-taught guitarist of gypsy background who lost two fingers in a caravan fire?

6 Who is the Argentinian-born clarinettist, tenor saxophonist, composer and multi jazz stylist who won the 'Grammy' for the soundtrack to 'Last Tango in Paris'?

7 Which Anglo-Indian clarinettist and composer was leader of the Fairweather All-Stars?

8 Who composed 'Round Midnight' and 'Straight, No Chaser'? He was often called the 'Prophet' and the 'High Priest' of bebop.

9 Who is celebrated in the history of jazz as the founder of the so-called 'Piano School of Harlem'?

10 Which Norwegian-born saxophonist's style is described as 'distilled thought'?

Inventors

1. Which Hungarian inventor produced the first ball-point pen in 1938?

2. What is the name of the valve containing an anode, a cathode and a control grid, that was invented in 1906 by L. De Forest?

3. What nationality was Geiger who gave his name to the Geiger counter?

4. With which invention is Alexander Graham Bell associated?

5. What is the surname of Robert, the American engineer who in the mid-1960s invented the electronic music synthesizer?

6. Which navigational instrument, invented by John Hadley in 1730, has an horizon glass and an index mirror?

7. Which thermoplastic material was invented by the American Hyatt brothers in 1870?

8. In 1884, which American-born inventor produced the first automatic machine gun?

9. Which American is best remembered for his invention of the cotton gin, a machine that separates cotton fibre from the seeds?

10. Which French oceanographer and movie-maker invented the aqualung?

Movies

1 Which 1954 movie starred Jane Wyman as a blind woman and Rock Hudson as the rich playboy responsible both for her blindness and its cure?

2 Which British actor made his U.S. movie debut as an Irish servant in 1916 Philadelphia in the 1967 Walt Disney movie 'The Happiest Millionaire'?

3 For their performances in which 1999 movie did James Coburn win an Oscar and Nick Nolte an Oscar nomination?

4 Which 1989 movie starred Richard Pryor as a blind man and Gene Wilder as a deaf man?

5 Who wrote and starred in the 1972 movie 'Play It Again Sam'?

6 Which 1990 movie starred Gene Hackman and Anne Archer as a deputy district attorney and his key witness?

7 Which legendary actor and dancer's first screen appearance came in 1933's 'Dancing Lady', in which he played himself?

8 Which 1989 baseball movie featured Tom Berenger and Charlie Sheen as team-mates?

9 Which actress took on the role of FBI agent Clarice Starling in the 2001 movie sequel 'Hannibal'?

10 Which actress played Sharon alongside David Duchovny's Randy in the 1991 movie about religious fanaticism, 'The Rapture'?

General Knowledge

1 Which American admiral of the Pacific campaign of World War II, has a class of aircraft carrier named after him?

2 Which nationalist group assassinated Spanish prime minister Luis Carrero Blanco in 1973?

3 The small European state of Montenegro was formerly part of which larger country?

4 What was the name of the uprisings, starting in 1987, by Palestinians in Israeli-occupied territories?

5 Who was the founder of the Holy Roman Empire?

6 In 2006, Forest Whitaker won an Oscar for his portrayal of which African despot?

7 Which actor founded the Sundance Film Festival?

8 Who was the daughter of King Ptolemy XII of Egypt?

9 Hans Christian Oersted, the first scientist to discover the connection between magnetism and electricity, was a native of which country?

10 What is measured on the Mohs Scale?

Geography

1 Which river has Vienna, Bratislava, Budapest and Belgrade along its course?

2 Which is the northernmost American state?

3 Which city on the river Danube is the capital of Upper Austria?

4 What is the southernmost of the four main islands of Japan?

5 Which large island is divided between Malaysia, Indonesia and Brunei?

6 What name is given to the hunters and gatherers who inhabited Australia before European settlement?

7 What name is given to the French-speaking inhabitants of Louisiana, whose ancestors were driven there from Acadia (Nova Scotia)?

8 Of which Canadian province is Fredericton the capital?

9 Which capital city is served by Schiphol airport?

10 In which European city is the Doge's Palace?

Literature

1 Who wrote 'The History of Mr Polly' and 'The Shape of Things to Come'?

2 Which French writer and dramatist was noted for his long nose and for fighting duels?

3 What was the third part of Arnold Wesker's trilogy that began with 'Chicken Soup with Barley'?

4 What term, attributed to Gertrude Stein, is applied to a group of disillusioned expatriate American writers in the 1920s?

5 Who wrote 'The Rape of the Lock' and 'The Dunciad'?

6 Which Hungarian author wrote the play 'Liliom' and the novel 'The Paul Street Boys'?

7 Which British author wrote 'The Hitchhiker's Guide to the Galaxy'?

8 'The Man of Property' is the first book in which sequence of novels by John Galsworthy?

9 Which British author wrote a series of medical novels including 'Doctor in the House'?

10 What nationality was the writer and environmental activist Ken Saro-Wiwa?

Art

1 In which country was the sculptor and woodcarver Grinling Gibbons born?

2 Van Gogh cut off part of his own left ear during a quarrel with which other artist?

3 What object is draped over the branch of a tree in Salvador Dali's painting 'The Persistence Of Memory'?

4 Which artist was appointed court painter to Charles IV of Spain in 1786?

5 Turkish-born Canadian portrait photographer Yousef Karsh, famous for his wartime studies of Churchill and other national leaders, signed himself as 'Karsh of ...' which city?

6 Which one of the seven deadly sins was portrayed in medieval art as a rider thrown from his horse?

7 'The Thinker' and 'The Kiss' are two famous works of which sculptor?

8 What nationality was the 17th century painter Jan Vermeer?

9 What was the artist Picasso's first name?

10 Which Italian artist and architect is supposed to have drawn a perfect circle as an example of his work in order to secure a Papal commission?

General Knowledge

1. What is meant by the acronym O.P.E.C.?

2. Who wrote 'The Great Gatsby'?

3. Which is the only play in which William Shakespeare mentions America?

4. The song 'Getting To Know You' comes from which musical?

5. In the early days of rock and roll who had a hit record with 'Shake, Rattle and Roll'?

6. What was the name of the teacher killed in the Challenger space shuttle explosion in January 1986?

7. Paradise Valley was the former name of which U.S. city?

8. What character did Mark Hamill play in 'Star Wars'?

9. What instrument did Jack Benny take on stage with him?

10. What type of books were written by the American novelist Zane Gray?

World War II: 1939

1 Which unarmed British passenger liner was sunk by a German U-boat on the first day of World War II?

2 Which German battleship was sunk off Montevideo after being chased there by British cruisers?

3 What was the name of the French defence line that followed the frontier between France and Germany?

4 The Soviet Union attacked which Nordic country in November 1939?

5 On 8th November, in which German city did Adolf Hitler escape a bomb blast?

6 Who was the prime minister of Britain at the start of the war?

7 What name was given to the German strategy of sudden and powerful attack?

8 Winston Churchill took up which British government appointment?

9 Early in 1939, Italy had invaded which Balkan country?

10 In November, to where did the Polish government-in-exile relocate?

The Animal Kingdom

1 What is the larva of a frog called?

_____

2 What type of creature is a gecko?

_____

3 What type of animal is a whaler?

_____

4 Which mammal of the family Odobenidae resembles a sea-lion?

_____

5 Which slow-moving South American mammal hangs upside down from branches feeding on leaves and fruit?

_____

6 Which land animal has the biggest eyes?

_____

7 Which creature is known as 'orange man' or 'wise man of the forest'?

_____

8 In the animal kingdom, what creature is otherwise known as the laughing jackass?

_____

9 Which nocturnal beetle emits a greenish light from organs on its abdomen?

_____

10 What are the only crustaceans adapted to living on land rather than water?

Food and Drink

1 What colour is absinthe, a potent aniseed-flavoured liqueur?

2 Uunijuusto, leipäjuusto, and lappi are all what types of food, originating in Finland?

3 Typically dried and salted, what kind of fish is traditionally used to make the Portuguese dish bacalao?

4 What name is given to a Greek white or rosé wine flavoured with resin?

5 Developed in Jamaica in the 1920s, an ortanique is a cross between which two citrus fruits?

6 Which nuts are traditionally used to flavour Bakewell Tart?

7 Which sauce is made of crushed basil leaves, pine nuts, garlic, Parmesan cheese, and olive oil, and is typically served with pasta?

8 Produced mainly in Burgundy, crème de cassis is a syrupy liqueur flavoured with which fruits?

9 From which country does the dessert tiramisu originate?

10 Kielbasa is a type of highly seasoned sausage, typically containing garlic, that originated from which country?

History

1 Where did Enola Gay say goodbye to her Little Boy in August 1945?

2 The U.S.A. purchased Alaska from which country in 1867?

3 During World War Two, which country fought against Russia in the separate Winter War of 1939-1940?

4 Olof Palme was the prime minister of which country when he was assassinated in 1986?

5 In August 1990, who invaded who, resulting in a war that followed early the next year?

6 The Great Influenza Pandemic of 1918-1920 is better known by which name?

7 In which year did the Bolshevik Revolution in Russia take place?

8 What was the name of the first man-made satellite to orbit Earth, in 1957?

9 In 1946, who coined the term 'Iron Curtain', meaning the dividing line between western Europe and the communist states to the east?

10 Who was the first president of the United States of America?

General Knowledge

1   The actual shape of our planet is described as an oblate spheroid; what does this term mean?

2   The caiman, of South America resembles which more commonly-known reptile?

3   Known formerly as Kampuchea and the Khmer Republic, what is this country's present-day name?

4   In which present-day African country was the Axum civilization located?

5   What is the name of the Israeli internal security service?

6   Which ancient Roman highway runs from Rome to the Adriatic port of Brindisi?

7   How many were the 'Labours of Hercules'?

8   The Chinese port of Macau is a former colony of which European country?

9   How many megatons explosive power was the largest-ever atomic bomb, the 'Tsar Bomb', detonated by Russia in 1961?

10   Which German former terrorist group was named after its two founder members?

Classical Music

1. Which orchestral piece by Richard Strauss gained widespread fame when it was used in the opening sequence to the movie '2001: A Space Odyssey'?

2. Who composed the oratorio 'A Child of Our Time' in 1945, inspired by the Nazi persecution of the Jews?

3. Who composed the 'Poeme Symphonique' in 1962 in which 100 wind-up metronomes tick away at different speeds, gradually winding down until there is only one, and then silence?

4. In which work by Jacques Ibert do you hear a policeman's whistle?

5. Who is the American composer of operas with a political theme, such as 'Nixon in China' or based on recent events, such as the hijacking of the ship 'Achille Lauro'?

6. Who, with Pavarotti and Domingo, is the third of the Three Tenors?

7. Claudio Abbado was principal conductor of the Berlin Philharmonic from 1990. Who succeeded him in 2002?

8. Whose famous Symphony No. 3 is known also as the 'Symphony of Sorrowful Songs'?

9. Which Russian-American violinist gave his first public performance in 1908 at seven years of age?

10. When a conductor faces a symphony orchestra are the cellos normally to his or her left or right?

Sport

1   Where and when were the first Summer Olympic Games held?

2   How long is the course of the Grand National horse race, held every year at Aintree?

3   Which U.S. tennis player formed a formidable partnership with Bob Lutz? Together they picked up several Doubles titles in the 1970s and 80s.

4   The 1998 Winter Olympics saw the introduction of curling, women's ice hockey and which other new event?

5   Football star, Edson Arantes do Nascimento, was better known by what name?

6   Which Australian swimmer won five medals; three gold, and one each of silver and bronze, at the 1972 Olympics?

7   Which British boxer floored Muhammad Ali at a fight in 1963; a shock that Ali recounted when he phoned his opponent 40 years later?

8   What are usual three endurance events that constitute the Triathlon?

9   The first of which kind of animal race was held at Hendon, near London, in 1876?

10 In 1993, at which tennis venue was player, Monica Seles stabbed by a spectator?

The Answer's a Country

1. The ringgit is the unit of currency in which country?

2. The Akita is a breed of dog originating from which country?

3. Romansch is an official language of which European country?

4. Which country's flag consists of a broad yellow horizontal stripe bordered by two narrower red horizontal stripes top and bottom?

5. In which country did the Sharpeville massacre take place?

6. Of which Baltic country is Riga the capital?

7. Which was the last country in Europe, as late as 1984, to give votes to women?

8. Scene of a daring rescue of hijacked airline passengers by Israeli troops in 1976, in which African country is the city of Entebbe?

9. In which North African country do the Berber people known as the Rif live?

10. From which country in South America does the monkey puzzle tree originate?

General Knowledge

1 True caviar is made from the eggs of which fish?

_____

2 Loudness, or sound-pressure, is measured in which units?

_____

3 Sirocco, mistral and foehn are all types of what?

_____

4 Which New York Stock Exchange index is the principal indicator of share price movements in the U.S.A.?

_____

5 Who starred as Bilbo Baggins in the 'Hobbit' films?

_____

6 Which Saudi Arabian city is the site of the tomb of the Prophet Muhammad?

_____

7 The ruined castle at Tintagel, Cornwall is said to be the birthplace of which legendary king of England?

_____

8 What is the former name of the Russian city of Volgograd?

_____

9 Which form of coal contains at least 92% carbon and burns without flame or smoke?

_____

10 King, Indian, Egyptian and Black-necked, are all species of which snake?

Mythology

1 In Greek mythology, who was the daughter of Cassiopeia and Cepheus?

_____

2 Which legendary magician was counsellor to King Arthur?

_____

3 Which character in Greek mythology fell in love with his own reflection?

_____

4 Who was the Roman equivalent of the Greek god Ares?

_____

5 According to Greek legend, which daughter of Minos helped Theseus to kill the Minotaur?

_____

6 According to Greek legend, what sort of monster was Medusa?

_____

7 What was the name of the Roman household gods associated with the storeroom?

_____

8 In Greek mythology, which daughter of Tantalus was turned into a weeping stone?

_____

9 In ancient times, which Greek mountain was held sacred to Apollo and the Muses?

_____

10 Name the ancient Greek warrior who was killed by a poisoned arrow shot into his heel.

Famous Ships

1 What was Admiral Nelson's flagship at the Battle of Trafalgar, that today is docked in Portsmouth as a museum ship?

2 On his famous expedition of 1492, Christopher Columbus' fleet of three ships comprised the 'Pinta', the 'Nina' and which other?

3 During the Falklands War of 1982, which Argentinian warship was torpedoed and sunk by a British submarine?

4 In 1872 which American cargo ship was found abandoned and drifting in the Atlantic, close to the Azores?

5 In 1989, which supertanker ran aground on the Alaskan coast, causing the spillage of eleven million gallons of oil?

6 Which American aircraft carrier holds the record as the world's longest naval vessel?

7 What was the world's first nuclear-powered submarine, launched in 1955?

8 The government of which country was responsible for the 1985 bombing of the Greenpeace ship, 'Rainbow Warrior' in Auckland harbour?

9 In 1945, which German ocean liner was sunk by a Russian submarine off the coast of Poland, killing over 9,000 people?

10 What do Britain's 'Mary Rose' and Sweden's 'Vasa' have in common?

Helio ...

1 Heliophobia is an irrational fear of what?

2 Heliopolis is a large suburb of which great Arabic city?

3 What name is given to the region of space that immediately surrounds the Sun?

4 In Greek mythology, what was the name of the personification of the Sun?

5 What name is given to a message transmitted by means of a mirror?

6 The name of which light gas is derived from the Greek word for 'sun'?

7 Which fragrant light purple/blue-flowered plant of the borage family is named after the Greek for 'sun'?

8 Which device was invented to enable an observer to look directly at the Sun without causing injury to the eye?

9 What name is given to the science of the study of the Sun?

10 Which Danish composer wrote the 'Helios Overture'?

Religion

1 In which African country did the Coptic Church originate?

2 In which month of the year is St. Patrick's Day celebrated?

3 The holy town of Lourdes is situated in the foothills of which mountain range?

4 Because he was entrusted with the 'keys of the Kingdom of Heaven', two crossed keys are the symbol of which apostle?

5 Which Spanish Jesuit missionary was known as the 'Apostle of the Indies'?

6 Which Indian river is the Hindus' most sacred river?

7 What was the name of the decree that granted religious freedom to the Huguenots in 1598?

8 What name was given to the religious revival in the American colonies during the 18th century that was inspired by the preaching of George Whitefield and Jonathan Edwards?

9 Adherence of which religion believes that Ahura Mazda, the good god, is in conflict with Ahriman, the evil god?

10 Which religion's most sacred books contain the teachings of Mahavira?

General Knowledge

1. What is meant by the Latin phrase 'caveat emptor'?

2. Which entertainer used the code name John Burrows and Dr. John Carpenter when answering telephone calls?

3. What was the name of the Ewing family Texas ranch in the TV series 'Dallas'?

4. What in Paris is the Bois De Boulogne?

5. Canadian singer Celine Dion won the 1988 Eurovision Song Contest for which country?

6. Which Shakespeare play is set in Elsinore Castle, Denmark?

7. What is the maximum number of clubs that a professional golfer is allowed to carry in his bag?

8. Who said: "Genius is 1% inspiration and 99% perspiration."?

9. Desdemona is a character in which Shakespeare play?

10. Who, after receiving bad reviews said: "I cried all the way to the bank."?

Science

1. How often does Halley's Comet visit the region of Earth?

_____

2. What name is given to a device that increases or decreases the voltage of alternating current?

_____

3. With which physicist is the formula E=MC squared associated?

_____

4. Which rare silvery metallic element has the symbol Yb?

_____

5. What name is given to a condition in which the temperature of the body is abnormally low?

_____

6. What is the Latin word for lead, from which the chemical symbol Pb is derived?

_____

7. Which red giant is the fourth brightest star in the sky?

_____

8. What measure of explosive power is equal to 1000 tons of TNT?

_____

9. Albert Einstein was offered the presidency of which country?

_____

10. What name is given to a device that enables computers to send and receive information via telephone?

History

1 Supposedly started by Mrs. O'Leary's cow kicking over an oil lamp, fire almost completely destroyed which U.S. city in 1871?

2 What name is given to the flight of Chinese communists to Yan'an, led by Mao Tse-tung?

3 Which guns were superseded by rifles in the mid-19th century?

4 The 60th anniversary of which battle was commemorated at Biggin Hill airfield near London in 2000?

5 In 1981, President Reagan announced the dismissal of 12,000 striking members of the PATCO trade union. What was their occupation?

6 Which medical condition, the name is no longer in technical use, was known in medieval times as the 'king's evil'?

7 Which famous Dublin theatre was established in 1904?

8 Which young Jewish girl is famous for the diary she kept while her family hid from the Nazis in Amsterdam?

9 Adolf Hitler was sent to prison in 1923 for attempting to overthrow the Bavarian government in which city?

10 On 6 December 1917, several munition ships exploded in the harbour of which Canadian port, killing over 1500 and making 20,000 people homeless?

Movies

1   Which 1995 comedy movie featured Bo Derek and Dan Aykroyd in cameo roles?

2   Who starred as the captain of the Soviet nuclear submarine in the 1990 movie 'The Hunt for Red October'?

3   Who starred as Doctor Dolittle in the 1967 movie?

4   Who played Stephen Biko in the 1987 movie 'Cry Freedom'?

5   Who sang the title track for the 1995 Bond movie 'GoldenEye'?

6   Which 1995 movie starred Demi Moore and Gary Oldman?

7   Which 1995 movie starred Leonardo DiCaprio as a sportsman turned performance poet?

8   Who directed the 1962 movie 'Lolita'?

9   Who played the female lead opposite Dudley Moore in the 1981 movie 'Arthur'?

10   Which actor died of a heart attack in 1967 shortly after completing his last movie 'Guess Who's Coming to Dinner'?

General Knowledge

1 Which is the largest island in the Mediterranean Sea?

_____

2 In economics, whose law states that: 'bad money drives out good money'?

_____

3 Is the denominator the upper or lower number of a fraction?

_____

4 What is the longest river in France?

_____

5 Which capital city is served by Haneda airport?

_____

6 Who was the five-and-a-half-inches tall boy in stories by the Brothers Grimm?

_____

7 Who is Snoopy's sister in the comic strip 'Peanuts'?

_____

8 Who was the youngest daughter of Tsar Nicolas II of Russia?

_____

9 Who were the first aviators to fly across the Atlantic non-stop?

_____

10 Who was the father of Alexander the Great?

Pop Music

1   Who sang the soundtrack to 'Even Cowgirls Get The Blues' in 1993?

_____

2   Who issued their 'BBC Sessions' in 1997?

_____

3   Who was 'Back To Front' in his 1992 album?

_____

4   Who could you have met in 1994 in their 'Voodoo Lounge'?

_____

5   Whose 1992 album promoted the idea of 'Love Deluxe'?

_____

6   Which group sang 'Urban Hymns' in 1997?

_____

7   In 1984 Madonna had her first really, really big hit ___?

_____

8   Prince made a splash in 1984 with his album ___?

_____

9   What are the names of the twins in the Bee Gees pop group?

_____

10   In 1976, which band were branded 'rotten punks' by the U.S. press, making them a symbol for punk rock?

Book Characters

1 Becky Sharp, George Osborne and Amelia Sedley feature in which novel?

2 Allan Quatermain is the central character in 'She', and other novels by which writer?

3 Holden Caulfield is the protagonist in which famous novel?

4 Which 'family' comprised parents William and Elizabeth, and sons Franz, Ernst, Jack and Fritz?

5 Daisy Buchanan is the object of the desires of the eponymous central character of which novel?

6 The dog, Buck, a collie-St Bernard cross is the central character in which novel by Jack London?

7 Hermione Granger and Ronald Weasley are important characters in which books?

8 David Bowman and Frank Poole are the two astronauts in which science-fiction novel?

9 Who is the knight's squire in the novel 'Don Quixote'?

10 Who was the secret agent (anonymous in the novels but named in the films based on them) in Len Deighton's 'The IPCRESS File', 'Funeral in Berlin' and 'The Billion Dollar Brain'?

Around the Islands

1 The Bass Strait separates the mainland of Australia from which Australian island?

_____

2 The Faroe Islands is a self-governing region of which European country?

_____

3 Which island is sometimes referred to as 'the teardrop of India'?

_____

4 Christmas Island in the Indian Ocean is a territory of which country?

_____

5 Of which Italian island is Cagliari the capital?

_____

6 With which Greek island do you associate the poet Sappho?

_____

7 The Bay of Pigs is on the south-west coast of which Caribbean country?

_____

8 Of which Mediterranean island is Nicosia the capital?

_____

9 Which is the most northerly of Japan's four main islands?

_____

10 Which Biblical king shares his name with a group of islands in the Pacific Ocean?

Geography

1 Of which U.S. state is Annapolis the capital?

2 In which European city can the Champs Élysées be found?

3 In which country did Queen Beatrix succeed her mother Queen Juliana in 1980?

4 Which diamond-mining city in South Africa is the capital of Northern Cape Province?

5 Which is the largest island of Japan?

6 Which Italian city is known as Firenze in Italian?

7 Of which Middle Eastern country is Amman the capital?

8 What is the ancient name of the peninsula occupied by Spain and Portugal?

9 Which sea-strait separates the North and South islands of New Zealand?

10 In which North African country is the town of Fez?

General Knowledge

1 Which actor husband of Elizabeth Taylor took his stage name from his school drama teacher?

2 What does the S stand for in Harry S. Truman?

3 Who wrote 'Elegy Written in a Country Churchyard'?

4 In which opera by Puccini does Lieutenant Pinkerton appear?

5 Who, in the title of a Shakespeare play, are Valentine and Proteus?

6 What is the collective name for a group of geese on land or in water?

7 What name is given to ice crystals formed from water vapour on windows, grass and other exposed surfaces near the ground?

8 Who wrote the play 'A Streetcar Named Desire'?

9 Ludwig von Koechel catalogued the works of which famous Austrian composer?

10 Boris Karloff received fourth billing at the end of which horror movie which premiered in 1931?

Literature

1 Which British novelist wrote 'My Cousin Rachel' and 'Rebecca'?

2 What were the first names of the poet T.S. Eliot?

3 What is the name of the young hero of Robert Louis Stevenson's 'Treasure Island'?

4 Which fictional detective is featured in 'A Study in Scarlet' and 'The Hound of the Baskervilles'?

5 Which work by Shakespeare do superstitious actors refer to as 'the Scottish play'?

6 Which American author wrote 'Breakfast at Tiffany's' and 'In Cold Blood'?

7 Which animals are the subject of Richard Adams' novel 'Watership Down'?

8 Which Canadian poet, novelist and singer-songwriter wrote 'Flowers for Hitler' and 'Beautiful Losers'?

9 Who wrote the children's novel 'Charlie and the Chocolate Factory'?

10 Who wrote the novels 'Our Man in Havana' and 'The Quiet American'?

Entertainment

1. Dale Evans, who died in February 2001, was the widow of which famous screen cowboy?

2. Which actor played James Bond in the 1974 movie 'The Man With the Golden Gun'?

3. Which dance is particularly associated with singer Chubby Checker?

4. Which American author created the Hardy Boys and Nancy Drew?

5. 'The Girl With Enamel Eyes' is the alternative title of which two-act ballet, first performed in Paris in 1870?

6. From which country does the dance known as the 'tarantella' originate?

7. What was the stage name of French-born movie actress Lily Claudette Chauchoin?

8. Actress Kate Hudson is the daughter of which actress?

9. Which high-kicking dance, performed by a female chorus, originated in the music halls of 19th century Paris?

10. Name the American-born cartoonist of the Monty Python comedy team.

The Human Body

1 Which visual defect is also called hyperopia or hypermetropia?

2 What name is given to the liquid part of blood?

3 What is the longest and largest artery in the body?

4 Which part of the human body is studied by a phrenologist?

5 A nephron is the functional unit of which organ in the human body?

6 What in the human body are classified by types known as 'true', 'false' and 'floating'?

7 What in the human body are affected by Paget's disease?

8 In which part of the human body is the fibula?

9 How many pairs of ribs are there in the human body?

10 Which flap of cartilage at the root of the tongue prevents food, etc., from entering the windpipe?

General Knowledge

1. Which group of Pacific Islands was once known as the Sandwich Islands?

2. British aviators, Alcock and Brown were the first to achieve which feat in 1919?

3. Charles Taylor is a former president of which African country?

4. Which present-day country was known as Cambria to the Romans?

5. What windspeed is represented by the number 12 on the Beaufort Scale?

6. What is the name for the written text of an opera?

7. How many strings does a balalaika have?

8. Who was assassinated by American forces at Abbottabad, Pakistan, on the 2nd of May 2011?

9. What is the name of the lower house of the Russian parliament?

10. How many countries comprised the original European Common Market?

History

1. In which American city was there a famous 'Tea Party' in 1773?

2. Which English explorer, who made three attempts to discover the Northwest Passage, gave his name to a bay on Baffin Island?

3. Which Germanic people invaded England, especially Kent, along with the Angles and Saxons in the 5th century A.D.?

4. What name is given to the hunters and gatherers who inhabited Australia before European settlement?

5. In 1969, who was the first person to set foot on the Moon?

6. Who became the first woman to serve as U.S. Attorney General in 1993?

7. Which South American Indian people ruled an empire centred on southern Peru?

8. Who succeeded Joseph Smith as leader of the Mormon church in 1844?

9. In the 1920s, Jan Smuts became prime minister of which country?

10. Which Wall Street guru was arrested in 1986 on a charge of insider trading, and obliged to pay a fine of 100 million dollars?

Politics

1   Who was the leader of East Germany from 1971 to 1989?

2   Who was the first Roman Catholic president of the United States?

3   In 1908 aged 3, what did Pu Yi become the last of?

4   What was ended by the 21st Amendment of the U.S. Constitution?

5   Who became the first U.S. unelected vice-president when he succeeded Spiro Agnew in 1973?

6   In which country is the Althing, the oldest parliament in the world?

7   Of which country was Gough Whitlam the prime minister during the 1970s?

8   Who, in 1988, became the first woman elected to govern a Muslim nation?

9   Who played J. Edgar Hoover in the movie 'Nixon'?

10   Who was the U.S. senator who became Elizabeth Taylor's seventh husband in 1976?

Sport

1 What was the nickname of Florence Griffith Joyner, U.S. athlete?

2 'The Great One' was a nickname bestowed on which Canadian athlete?

3 Which French skier became the first World Cup champion in 1967 and took three gold medals at the Winter Olympics the following year?

4 Basketball ace, Kareem Abdul-Jabbar played himself disguised as a co-pilot, in which film?

5 Who, in 1998, became the youngest football player in an England international team?

6 Muhammad Ali famously changed his name from what, in 1964?

7 Which Australian tennis ace won the Ladies Singles titles in 1971 and 1980?

8 Which is the premier horse race of the Australian racing season?

9 What is the nickname of former basketball player, Earvin Johnson?

10 Which Italian was the first-ever driver to win a Formula One World Championship, in 1950?

Astrology

1 Jon Dee was an astrologer whose services were engaged by which English monarch?

2 The word 'zodiac' comes from ancient Greece. What does it mean?

3 Someone born at Christmas will fall under which star sign?

4 'Tetrabiblos' was a work on the subject of astrology written by Claudius Ptolemy in around 150 A.D. What does Tetrabiblos mean?

5 The earliest evidence of the practice of astrology was found to date back to around 3000 B.C.; in which present-day country?

6 How does the word 'astrology' translate into English from its original Latin?

7 In astrology, which term denotes being born at the point where one sign changes to another?

8 Which First Lady of the U.S.A. commissioned an astrologer after the attempted assassination of her husband in 1981?

9 How many degrees are there in a house?

10 In the table of astrological symbols, which celestial body is represented by a solid black disc inside a black circle?

General Knowledge

1. Invented in the mid nineteenth century, Parkesine was the first kind of which material?

2. Which English campaigner for women's rights threw herself in front of King George V's horse at the Epsom Derby Race in 1913, dying from her injuries four days later?

3. Twenty million of which exotic sea creatures are pointlessly killed each year for use in Chinese 'medicine'?

4. Which word can refer to the Morning Star, a friction-ignited match and an evil biblical figure?

5. Which Greek god is the equivalent of the Roman god, Mercury?

6. In mysticism, who are Camael, Cassiel, Uriel and Hagiel?

7. In the Bible, which kind of birds appeared in order to provide meat to the Israelites during their flight from Egypt?

8. In the ballet 'Checkmate', the white animated chess pieces represent Love; what do the black pieces represent?

9. In 1994, Nancy Kerrigan was attacked and disabled in order to prevent her from competing in which sport?

10. Which alcoholic drink is sold in bottle sizes named after Biblical characters?

Music

1   Who wrote the opera 'Tosca'?

2   Which numbered train engine is mentioned in the song, 'On the Atchison, Topeka and the Santa Fe'?

3   In 1987, Joe Cocker had a big hit with ___?

4   Which British soloist's album, issued in 1988, was 'The Shouting Stage'?

5   Which famous composer had an affair with French novelist George Sand?

6   Which group issued an album in 1988 advising you to 'Blow Up Your Video'?

7   'Summertime' is a song from which George Gershwin opera?

8   Which group, in 1987, went 'Through The Looking-glass'?

9   Which group sang 'Live Under A Blood Red Sky' in 1983?

10 Whose 'Symphony No. 41 in C' is known as the 'Jupiter'?

Rivers

1   The Tigris and Euphrates rivers meet in which country?

_____

2   Which is Africa's second-longest river?

_____

3   Which river of North America connects the Great Lakes to the Atlantic Ocean?

_____

4   Into which sea does the river Rhône flow?

_____

5   The capital cities of Austria, Slovakia, Hungary and Serbia all stand on which major river?

_____

6   Which is the longest river of the British Isles?

_____

7   Into which inland sea does the River Volga flow?

_____

8   Which river forms much of the boundary between the U.S. and Mexico?

_____

9   Which two South American capital cities stand on the Rio de la Plata estuary on the Atlantic Ocean?

_____

10   The rivers Lena and Yenisei flow into the Arctic Ocean on the shores of which country?

ROUND 129

Crime

1. When Johnny Cash entertained the inmates of San Quentin prison, a future country singer was in the audience serving time for burglary. Can you name him?

2. Who in 1876 was shot in the back by Jack McCall while holding a 'Dead Man's Hand' at poker?

3. Albert De Salvo is notoriously better known by what nickname?

4. What was the nickname of the American outlaw Robert LeRoy Parker?

5. Which one of the James Brother's wild west outlaw gang died peacefully at the age of 72, never having been convicted of a crime?

6. The final words of which American gangster and racketeer were: "The bullet hasn't been made that can kill me"?

7. Who was the granddaughter of William Randolph Hearst kidnapped by the SLA in 1974?

8. In what type of building did the St. Valentine's Day massacre take place?

9. Which group issued an album in 1987 entitled 'Strangeways, Here We Come'?

10. By what name was Theodore Kaczynski, jailed for life for a series of terrorist attacks, known?

General Knowledge

1. What sort of gemstone is the jewel known as the Koh-i-noor?

2. Which Australian marsupial is also called a banded anteater?

3. Which slow-moving arboreal mammal of South and Central America hangs upside down from branches feeding on leaves and fruit?

4. Name the loose-fitting garment consisting of a piece of cloth draped around the body and worn by the citizens of ancient Rome.

5. In February 1996, Joan Collins won a New York court case against which book publishers?

6. How is 19 written in Roman numerals?

7. What type of creatures are the eastern diamondback and fer-de-lance?

8. DCL are the Roman numerals for what number?

9. Which breed of spotted dog is named after an Adriatic coastal region?

10. Originating in Latin America, what name is given to the dance consisting of three steps and a kick to each bar performed by a number of people in single file?

ROUND 131

Movies

1. Who played Billie Holiday in the 1972 movie 'Lady Sings the Blues'?

2. Who directed the 1995 Bond movie 'GoldenEye'?

3. Who played the President's girlfriend in the 1995 movie 'The American President'?

4. Which actress played the title role in the 1983 movie 'Silkwood'?

5. In 1996 a Swiss museum paid £44,750 for a bowler hat and cane belonging to which silent movie star?

6. Which English actress and model starred in the 1997 movie 'Austin Powers: International Man of Mystery'?

7. Which 1988 Alan Parker movie starred Gene Hackman and Willem Dafoe as FBI agents?

8. Who played Iago in Oliver Parker's movie version of 'Othello'?

9. Who played Caesar to Elizabeth Taylor's Cleopatra in the 1963 blockbuster movie?

10. Which 1992 movie starring Tom Hanks, Geena Davis and Madonna tells the story of The All-American Girl's Professional League?

Nature

1. Which birds fly in groups called 'skeins'?

2. What is the name given to subsoil that is permanently frozen?

3. What name is given to an optical illusion such as of an oasis in a desert?

4. What is the anatomical name for the lower jawbone?

5. Which gas needed by green plants is released into the atmosphere by animals during respiration?

6. Which member of the cat family is also called an ounce?

7. What name is given to an earthed metal rod placed at the top of a tall building?

8. Which African mammal has a name which means 'earth pig' in Afrikaans?

9. Mount Egmont is a major volcanic peak in which country?

10. To which sea area in the North Atlantic do eels migrate each year to breed?

The Bible

1   Who, in the Bible, performed the 'Dance of the Seven Veils'?

2   What are the names of the Four Horsemen of the Apocalypse?

3   In the Bible, which king was the son of David and Bathsheba?

4   For how many years in Genesis 5:27 was Methuselah said to have lived?

5   In the Old Testament, which two cities of Palestine were known as the cities of the plain?

6   Which of the disciples of Jesus was the brother of Andrew, and a fisherman?

7   Who was the son of Isaac and the brother of Esau?

8   Who was the beggar in Jesus' parable of the rich man and the poor man?

9   According to the Bible, how many loaves did Jesus use to feed the five thousand?

10 According to the sermon on the mount, who shall 'inherit the Earth'?

History

1 The failed Gunpowder plot of 1605 was partly an assassination attempt on which English king?

2 Which volcano was responsible for the destruction of Pompeii in 79 A.D.?

3 Which former country disintegrated into civil war after the death of its dictator Marshal Tito in 1980?

4 The Cod War, a series of disputes over fishing rights, was fought by Britain against which country in the 1950s/60s?

5 Which U.S. senator was largely responsible for the anti-communist hysteria which affected America from 1947 to 1954?

6 Which cleric led the revolution which overthrew the Shah of Iran in 1979?

7 Which Asian territory was acquired by Britain in 1841?

8 Suleiman the Magnificent became the Sultan of which country in 1520?

9 Explorer, John Cabot discovered which territory, now part of Canada, in 1497?

10 In which year did Christopher Columbus make his first voyage and accidentally discover the New World?

General Knowledge

1. In which country is the Wieliczka salt mine, that contains an entire town below ground, where everything from stairs to chandeliers is made from salt?

2. What colour are the berries of the mistletoe plant?

3. A typical snowflake has how many sides (or 'arms')?

4. What is 0.0625 when expressed as a fraction?

5. The longest bridge in Europe, in which country is the Vasco da Gama Bridge?

6. Which sci-fi author's third law states that "Any sufficiently advanced technology is indistinguishable from magic"?

7. The volcano Mount Etna is on which island?

8. What is the capital of Romania?

9. What is the cube root of 512?

10. Which country has the international vehicle registration code letters RA?

Art

1. Which 15th century German artist, especially famed for his engravings, created the 'Apocalypse' series of woodcuts?

2. Which famous painting by Edvard Munch was stolen from museums in 1994 and 2004?

3. Who painted the famous 'Laughing Cavalier'?

4. 'The Garden of Earthly Delights' is a three-part painting by which Dutch master?

5. Which former Paris railway station today houses an art museum?

6. 'Wheat field with Crows' 'Irises' and 'Cherry tree' are paintings by which artist?

7. Michaelangelo, Donatello and Bernini all produced works of art based on which biblical figure?

8. Which French artist created many paintings on the subject of ballet dancers, and is especially noted for his 'L'Absinthe' of 1876?

9. Which 18th-19th century German romantic artist created many surreal paintings such as 'The Wanderer Above the Sea of Fog' and the chaotic 'Sea of Ice'?

10. Which early 20th century art movement was named after a painting by one of the movement's founders, Wassily Kandinsky?

Geography

1 Which European lake is also known as Lac Léman?

2 Which channel separates New Zealand's North Island and South Island?

3 What is the state capital of Connecticut, U.S.A.?

4 Of which African country is Mogadishu the capital?

5 Which U.S. city is served by O'Hare International airport?

6 What is the largest city, and the financial capital, of Switzerland?

7 In which present-day European country is composer Gustav Mahler's birthplace?

8 What is the second largest of the Great Lakes of North America?

9 In which country are the Sierra Madre mountains?

10 Lake Erie forms most of the northern boundary of which American state?

Physics

1 Heat flows from a hotter to a colder body, not the reverse, is the simplified second law of what?

_____

2 What is the SI unit measure of electrical resistance?

_____

3 Plasma is one of the fundamental states of matter; what are the other three?

_____

4 What is the SI unit of force?

_____

5 Which optical device causes light to converge or diverge?

_____

6 What term describes the lowest limit on the temperature scale; minus 273.15 degrees Celsius?

_____

7 What hypothetical nuclear reaction would take place at low temperatures as opposed to the extremely high temperatures required for nuclear reaction?

_____

8 What is the SI scale for temperature?

_____

9 What property of a liquid describes its resistance to flow?

_____

10 Whose Third Law of Motion states that 'to every action there is an equal and opposite reaction'?

General Knowledge

1 The Bechuanaland Protectorate became the Republic of (what) in September 1966?

2 What name is given to the ridges on the neck of a guitar or other instrument which divide the fingerboard into spaces producing different notes?

3 What nationality are the brewery companies Carlsberg and Fuglsang?

4 Which country has the international telephone dialling code 39?

5 A cotton-stuffed mattress laid out on the floor for use as a bed, the word 'futon' is derived from which language?

6 Of which country was Dilma Rouseff elected president in 2011?

7 Who wrote the plays 'A Doll's House', 'The Wild Duck' and 'Hedda Gabler'?

8 What is the name of the bulldog who features in Tom and Jerry cartoons?

9 In Scandinavian mythology, what name is given to the place in which heroes killed in battle were believed to feast with Odin for eternity?

10 The Golden Calf, an animal with 18-carat gold horns and hooves, preserved in formaldehyde, is the work of which artist?

Classical Music

1 Who composed the ballet 'Appalachian Spring' for which he received the 1945 Pulitzer Prize?

_____

2 Who composed the music for the ballets 'The Sleeping Beauty' and 'Swan Lake'?

_____

3 Who composed the music for the ballets 'Coppelia' and 'Sylvia'?

_____

4 Who composed the music for the ballet 'Cinderella'?

_____

5 Who composed the music for the ballets 'The Rite of Spring', 'The Fire Bird' and 'Petrouchka'?

_____

6 Who composed the music for the ballet 'Prelude a L'Apres-Midi d'un Faune'?

_____

7 Who composed the music for the ballet 'The Three Cornered Hat'?

_____

8 Who composed the music for the ballet 'Les Sylphides'?

_____

9 Who wrote the opera 'The Magic Flute'?

_____

10 The 'Dance of the Sugar Plum Fairy' is part of which Tchaikovsky ballet?

Travel and Transport

1 On which ill-fated Transatlantic ocean liner was William Murdoch first officer?

_____

2 What in aviation is meant by the abbreviation, STOL?

_____

3 Which ship carried the Pilgrim Fathers to America?

_____

4 What was the name of the Illinois Central express on which Casey Jones lost his life in 1900?

_____

5 The 'Cutty Sark' is a famous ship now moored at Greenwich in London. In the 18th century this ship was used to bring which product from China?

_____

6 Which 61-mile-long canal links the Baltic and North Seas?

_____

7 What nautical measurement is the speed of one sea-mile per hour?

_____

8 What is the name given to travellers in a group or convoy, especially through a desert?

_____

9 In which sea did the Russian submarine the 'Kursk' sink in 2000?

_____

10 Which bridge over the River Thames in London has a central section that can be raised to allow ships to pass?

Sport

1 Who became the world's top female tennis player when she beat Serena Williams at the 2004 Wimbledon Final?

2 The Uber Cup is awarded in which sport?

3 Who was the first female gymnast to be awarded a perfect ten score at her appearance at the 1976 Olympics?

4 When was the U.S. Major League baseball strike that cost the sport an entire season?

5 On which piece of equipment would a gymnast perform a 'giant swing'?

6 Which country won the Fifa World Cup in 2010?

7 Which series of games is similar in scope to the Olympics but involves only the countries of North, South and Central America?

8 Former snooker player, Cliff Thorburn is a native of which country?

9 Who was Sweden's only World Heavyweight boxing champion?

10 Which team won the first two U.S. football Superbowl events (1967 and 1968)?

Literature

1 In 'Gone With the Wind', by what name did her father always refer to Scarlett O'Hara?

_____

2 Who wrote 'Fahrenheit 451' and 'I Sing the Body Electric'?

_____

3 Who marries Katherine in Shakespeare's 'The Taming of the Shrew'?

_____

4 What is the pen name of David Cornwell?

_____

5 Which English poet and dramatist wrote 'The Beggar's Opera'?

_____

6 Who founded the Académie Française to preserve the purity of the French language?

_____

7 Which U.S. author created Brer Rabbit and Brer Fox?

_____

8 Which U.S. dramatist wrote the plays 'American Buffalo' and 'Glengarry Glen Ross'?

_____

9 Who wrote the 'Death of a Salesman' and 'A View From The Bridge'?

_____

10 Miranda and Caliban are both characters in which play by Shakespeare?

General Knowledge

1. Which town in central Spain (which gave its name to an industrial city in Ohio) is famous for its swords and knives?

2. What are 'close encounters of the second kind'?

3. Is 'nyctaphobia' the fear of darkness, dirt or poverty?

4. The language Afrikaans derives from which European language?

5. Thought to be the first of its kind, what was the German, 'Avisa Relation oder Zeitung', which appeared in 1609?

6. Which is the shortest modern European alphabet, with only 21 letters?

7. What is the motto of the Special Air Service (SAS) division of the British Army?

8. Who was the American journalist who was held hostage in Lebanon for 2,454 days, finally being freed in 1991?

9. What was the former method of execution in Spain by means of strangling or breaking the neck with an iron collar?

10. What is meant by the Latin phrase 'a tergo'?

The Animal Kingdom

1. What are the organs of locomotion and balance in fishes called?

2. What name is given to the burrowing crab with an enlarged claw that it holds like a violin?

3. Which aquatic bird has Canada, barnacle and greylag varieties?

4. The dark-reddish brown pigment obtained from the inky secretion of cuttlefish and used as a dye and an ink since Roman times is called what?

5. Which large venomous African viper is noted for inflating its body when alarmed?

6. What type of creature is a fulmar?

7. What sort of creatures transmit Lyme disease?

8. What is a female fox called?

9. To which animals does the adjective 'feline' refer?

10. The marabou stork is native to which continent?

History

1. Prior to being called The White House, by what name was the U.S. president's dwelling known?

2. How was Manfred von Richthofen better known in World War I?

3. Which famous train ran from Cincinnati to New Orleans?

4. At 69 years old who was the oldest American president to take office?

5. Who did Hillary Rodham marry in 1975?

6. Which Roman emperor died after eating poisoned mushrooms given to him by his wife Agrippina?

7. To which island was Napoleon Bonaparte exiled after his defeat at the Battle of Waterloo?

8. The border between which two countries was set at the 49th parallel in 1818?

9. In which South American country was Che Guevara shot and killed?

10. Which American president fired General Douglas McArthur in 1951?

Mythology

1   In Greek mythology, who was the legendary lover of Hero who swam across the Hellespont each night?

2   In Greek mythology, which handsome youth was loved by Aphrodite?

3   Which ancient Roman festival honoured the God of agriculture?

4   In Greek mythology, who was the wife of Agamemnon and mother of Orestes?

5   In Greek mythology, who was the Muse of history?

6   In Greek mythology, which nymph was changed into a laurel tree to escape from Apollo?

7   Who was the supreme god in Greek mythology?

8   Which many-headed monster was killed by Hercules as one of his labours?

9   In medieval legend, which creature could only be captured by a virgin putting its head in her lap?

10 In Greek legend, which dog guarded the entrance to the underworld?

General Knowledge

1 Which member of the Beach Boys drowned, aged 39, in 1983?

2 In which U.S. state did the Wounded Knee massacre of Sioux Indians take place in 1890?

3 The name of which city in South America means 'Vale of Paradise'?

4 What is the meaning of the French term 'haute couture'?

5 What is another name for the card game 'chemin de fer'?

6 In which country did tarot cards originate?

7 What is the name of the lace shawl worn over the head and shoulders by Spanish women?

8 What nationality was the philosopher Immanuel Kant?

9 What is the meaning of the phrase 'cri de coeur'?

10 What Latin phrase, meaning 'bounteous mother' is used of universities and schools?

War

1 Which Italian soldier and patriot won Sicily and Naples for the new kingdom of Italy?

2 Which country was invaded by Iraq in 1990, leading to the Gulf War?

3 Which leading German World War II rocket engineer worked for the U.S. Army and N.A.S.A. after the war?

4 What was the nickname of the American Confederate general Thomas Jackson?

5 Which 1959 movie starred Frank Sinatra as the commander of a British-American task force in Burma during World War II?

6 After World War I, Transylvania became part of which country?

7 In which German prison was Rudolf Hess imprisoned up to his death in 1987?

8 Which U.S. general was nicknamed Black Jack, and gave his name to a nuclear missile?

9 What type of bomb is an 'enhanced radiation weapon'?

10 Which World War II battle is also known as the Ardennes Offensive?

Food and Drink

1 Which cocktail consists of rye whiskey and sweet vermouth?

_____

2 Which cheese is traditionally grated and sprinkled on spaghetti?

_____

3 What is the name of the very spicy Italian sausage eaten hot or cold?

_____

4 Which Greek philosopher died by drinking hemlock?

_____

5 Vinho Verdi is a white wine from which country?

_____

6 The wine 'marsala' comes from which region of Italy?

_____

7 In cookery, florentine means food served with which vegetable?

_____

8 Which annual cereal grass is grown in paddy fields?

_____

9 Coeliac disease is caused by an intolerance to gliadin, a component of which protein found in wheat?

_____

10 What is the name of the Japanese dish of vinegared rice with raw fish?

Movies

1 Which 1981 movie about 17th century Japanese political intrigue starred Richard Chamberlain as a shipwrecked Englishman?

2 Which 1963 movie starring Doris Day and James Garner was a remake of 1940's 'My Favorite Wife', starring Cary Grant and Irene Dunne?

3 Which movie starred Sharon Stone as the mother of a hunchback boy and Gillian Anderson as a biker's moll?

4 In which 1968 movie did Jim Brown and Gene Hackman star as leaders of a convict revolt in Arizona State Prison?

5 Which 1987 Coen brothers' movie starred Nicolas Cage and Holly Hunter as a couple who steal a baby?

6 Which late actor played the young Indiana Jones in the 1989 movie 'Indiana Jones and the Last Crusade'?

7 Keenan Ivory Wayans wrote, directed and starred in which 1994 comedy movie about a falsely disgraced cop?

8 In Gus Van Sant's 1999 version of 'Psycho', which actress played Janet Leigh's role of Marion Crane?

9 Who wrote the novels on which the movies 'Grand Hotel' and 'Hotel Berlin' were based?

10 Which Australian actress played a single mother with powers of extra-sensory perception in the 2000 movie 'The Gift'?

Pop Music

1 'Bye Bye Love' was an early hit for ___?

_____

2 What was the name of the album brought out in 1995 by Black Sabbath?

_____

3 Who asked us to 'Keep The Faith' in 1992?

_____

4 Who was the 'Earthling' in 1997?

_____

5 Which charismatic lady issued an album in 1991 complaining that 'Love Hurts'?

_____

6 Whose 1994 album showed clearly what he had been doing since he leapt 'From The Cradle'?

_____

7 In 1997 Fleetwood Mac returned to issue an album which was actually an invitation to what?

_____

8 Which ageing Welsh heart-throb proved he was still capable of 'Carrying a Torch' in 1991?

_____

9 Which American group brought out the album 'Good Stuff' in 1992?

_____

10 Which much admired lady warned us that she was 'The Force Behind The Power' in 1991?

General Knowledge

1 Who were the opposing countries in the Battle of Bunker Hill?

2 What in Russia is 'Izvestia'?

3 Sam Phillips, the music producer whose career was intertwined with that of Elvis Presley, founded which record label?

4 The name of what, in Australia, is derived from an Aborigine word for 'I don't understand'?

5 'Everything I Do (I Do It For You)' sung by Bryan Adams is the theme song from which movie?

6 Addis Ababa is the capital of which African country?

7 What is the most common Spanish surname?

8 Of which actor did Howard Hughes remark that his ears made him look like a taxi cab with both doors open?

9 What is the common name of Beethoven's Symphony No. 3 in E flat?

10 The Peninsular War of 1808 to 1814 was fought on which peninsula?

Science Fiction

1. Which SF writer created the characters Elric, Hawkmoon, and Jerry Cornelius and wrote 'The Dancers at the End of Time' series of SF novels?

2. Which 2002 Steven Spielberg SF film based on a story by Philip K Dick, starred Tom Cruise as Captain John Anderton, a 'PreCrime' detective?

3. 'Rendezvous with Rama' is a 1972 best-selling novel by which author?

4. 'Ice Nine' is a lethal material which appears in which Kurt Vonnegut's novel?

5. 'The Drowned World', 'The Burning World', and 'The Crystal World' are by which author?

6. Who wrote the 'Helliconia' Trilogy?

7. Which famous title by Frank Herbert has become the world's best-selling SF novel?

8. Which famous novel by Walter M Miller Jr. is set in a monastery in post-nuclear war America?

9. What is the better-known name of the English SF author who sometimes wrote under the names John Beynon and Lucas Parkes?

10. What was the original British title for the John Christopher novel published in the U.S. as 'No Blade of Grass'?

Language

1. Apart from French, German and Romansch, what is the other official language of Switzerland?

2. What was the language of ancient Rome?

3. In language, what word means the use of words starting with the same letter or sound, for example big black box?

4. Sanskrit was an old literary language of which country?

5. From which language is the word 'helicopter' derived?

6. What is the official language of Paraguay?

7. What Y is a compound language of Hebrew and German?

8. Which English word for a type of single-storey dwelling is derived from the Gujarati word meaning 'of Bengal'?

9. Which saint is the reputed inventor of the alphabet used in Russian and other Slavic languages?

10. Which country is known as Suomi in its native language?

Science

1 Which synthetic fibre was introduced commercially in 1938?

_____

2 Who, in 1928, discovered penicillin?

_____

3 Which Nobel prize was won by Albert Einstein in 1955?

_____

4 Edward Jenner discovered a vaccine for which disease?

_____

5 What name is given to drugs that increase the output of urine by the kidneys?

_____

6 Which metallic chemical element is also known as wolfram?

_____

7 Which branch of medicine deals with the diagnosis and treatment of disorders of the heart?

_____

8 What is the smallest unit of fluid measure in the apothecaries' system of measurement?

_____

9 Which allergic condition is also called nettle rash and hives?

_____

10 In which American city was the potentially deadly Legionnaires' disease first identified?

General Knowledge

1 Who created the fictional detective Hercule Poirot?

2 'The Brabanconne' is the national anthem of which country?

3 Becky Sharpe is a character in which novel?

4 Which cartoon character was introduced in 1929 by E. C. Segar in his 'Thimble Theater' comic strip?

5 Malev is the airline of which eastern European country?

6 Which U.S. state has the highest number of people?

7 First proposed by Ronald Reagan, for what is SDI an acronym?

8 What is the name of the white-faced character created by the French mime-artist Marcel Marceau?

9 A native of South Africa, what type of creature is a marabou?

10 Winnipeg is the capital of which Canadian province?

History

1. Whom did Mark David Chapman shoot and kill on 8th December, 1980?

2. Which 'first' was achieved by Reinhold Messner when he climbed Mount Everest in 1980?

3. What was the nickname of the German general Erwin Rommel?

4. Which Bolshevik leader was assassinated in Mexico in 1940?

5. Who was the leader of the Khmer Rouge who took power in Cambodia in 1975?

6. Which king of France was the husband of Catherine de' Medici?

7. In which Texas city was President John F. Kennedy assassinated in 1963?

8. Which major naval battle was fought on October 21st, 1805?

9. Which Asian country was divided into North and South in 1954?

10. Who was vice-president under Dwight D. Eisenhower?

Geography

1. Point Marroqui is the most southerly point of which continent?

2. What was the former name of the Zimbabwean capital Harare?

3. Of which European country is Piraeus the chief port?

4. Of which country is Table Mountain a famous landmark?

5. Of which Mediterranean island is Palermo the capital?

6. What is the state capital of Colorado?

7. Of which American state is Juneau the capital?

8. What mountain range is known as 'the backbone of Italy'?

9. In which African country is the town of Timbuktu, or Tombouctou?

10. What name is given to the region around the North Pole?

Religion

1 Who was the first Holy Roman emperor?

_____

2 In the Bible, who was the first king of Israel?

_____

3 Who succeeded Joseph Smith as head of the Mormon Church?

_____

4 Which Spanish priest founded the Society of Jesus, commonly known as the Jesuits?

_____

5 In the Bible, who was found in the bull rushes by Pharaoh's daughter?

_____

6 What is the main religion of Japan?

_____

7 In the Bible, who is the father of David?

_____

8 Who, in the Bible, was the first person to be born?

_____

9 In the Bible, whose brother was Aaron?

_____

10 Who is the patron saint of lost causes?

Rulers and Leaders

1   Name the British general who died leading his men in the capture of Quebec in 1759.

2   Genghis Khan and his grandson Kublai Khan were leaders of which race of Asiatic people?

3   Which king of Lydia was famous for his immense wealth?

4   Which American president was assassinated in 1901?

5   Which French statesman became the premier for the second time in 1917 at the age of 76?

6   Name the Chinese leader who was ousted by the Communists in 1949. He fled to Formosa, now Taiwan, where he established the Republic of China.

7   Of which country was Sukarno the first president?

8   Which Roman emperor was assassinated in the Senate House on the Ides of March?

9   Who came to power on 1 January 1959 when he overthrew the government led by Fulgencio Batista?

10   Carlos Menem, Leopoldo Galtieri and Juan Peron have all been presidents of which country?

General Knowledge

1 Genophobia is the fear of what?

2 Which constellation is named after the many-headed serpent killed by Hercules?

3 Which sea passage separates the South Atlantic from the South Pacific?

4 What kind of astronomical phenomena are represented by the Geminids, Leonids and Perseids?

5 Which American writer, noted for his 'Devil's Dictionary' disappeared in 1914, his fate being unknown to this day?

6 New York, London, Berlin, Moscow: which is furthest south?

7 The Galilean Satellites are the four major moons of which planet?

8 Which country has the world's longest railway network?

9 In the cartoon series, who was Dick Dastardly's muttering canine sidekick?

10 Zane Grey is best known for which genre of fictional literature?

The Olympics

1. At which event did Al Oerter win four gold medals at successive Olympic games?

2. Which U.S. track star won four gold medals at the 1936 Berlin Olympics?

3. At which sport did Irina Rodnina win Olympic gold medals in 1972, 1976 and 1980?

4. Which former Olympic and World Skating Champion starred in the 1995 television movie 'The Ice Princess'?

5. Where was the venue of the 1994 Winter Olympics?

6. Which was the first American city to host the modern Olympic Games?

7. Which country always leads the Olympic procession at the opening ceremony?

8. What name is given to the period of four years between each Olympic Games?

9. Which famous sportsman was presented with a gold medal during the 1996 Olympics to replace the one he threw away in the 1960s?

10. In what year did beach volleyball become an Olympic sport?

Lakes

1 Lake Neusiedl stands on the frontier between Austria and which other country?

2 In which American state is Lake Okeechobee?

3 Which is the smallest of the Great Lakes of North America?

4 The U.S. cities of Cleveland and Buffalo stand on the shore of which one of the Great Lakes?

5 Which Swiss resort lies between the lakes of Brienz and Thun?

6 Lake Inari is the largest lake of the northern part of which European country?

7 Which lake of South America is the world's highest-altitude navigable lake?

8 The Canadian city of Toronto stands on the shore of which of the Great Lakes?

9 Which Swiss city, the country's second-largest, stands on Lac Leman?

10 Which inland sea of Central Asia has, due to water diversions for irrigation elsewhere, shrunk by more than 90% since 1960?

Music

1. The name of what piece of music means, literally, an opening?

2. What adjective pertains to the 'Muse of Dancing'?

3. How many prongs has a tuning fork?

4. Which famous rock festival took place in New York state in August 1969?

5. Which musical instrument was the focus of a 1999 movie featuring Samuel L. Jackson and Greta Scacchi, which followed its story from 17th century Italy to modern Canada?

6. The Spaniard, Andres Segovia was a virtuoso on which instrument?

7. What were the Guarneri family famous for making?

8. In a symphony orchestra, which is the only stringed instrument that is not played with a bow?

9. Name the American saxophonist and singer (who died aged 53 in 1995) who fronted the All-Stars.

10. Which U.S. comic actor played a Russian circus musician in the 1984 movie 'Moscow on the Hudson'?

General Knowledge

1. Which German-born British astronomer wrote over twenty symphonies and many other classical compositions?

2. Who played the part of Dr. McCoy in the original TV series of 'Star Trek'?

3. Snorri Sturluson was a 12th-13th century poet and historian of which island country?

4. The Dogger Bank is located in which sea?

5. Which American astronomer (1855-1916), who founded the observatory that bears his name at Flagstaff, Arizona, was convinced of the existence of 'canals' on Mars?

6. Which stage work by Oscar Wilde inspired Richard Strauss to write an opera of the same name that shocked audiences with its 'Dance of the Seven Veils'?

7. Johann Wolfgang von Goethe wrote which tragic play based on a legendary figure who makes a pact with the devil?

8. Which is Australia's longest river?

9. Who was the wife of the Egyptian god, Osiris?

10. Which metal has the highest coefficient of conductivity?

Science

1 Which metallic element has the property of catching fire if dropped in hot water?

2 Which silvery-white metallic element has the symbol Pd?

3 What V is a finely calibrated scale named after a 17th century French mathematician?

4 What colour does blue litmus turn in the presence of acid?

5 What name is given to the science of the physical laws according to which projectiles move in flight?

6 Which term describes the amount of water vapour in the air?

7 Who, in 1988, wrote the scientific book 'A Brief History of Time'?

8 AOL is an internet service provider. What do the letters AOL stand for?

9 Which Soviet physicist and dissident was awarded the Nobel Peace Prize in 1975?

10 Which unstable radioactive element has the symbol At?

Literature

1   What was the pen name of French playwright Jean Baptiste Poquelin?

2   For which novel was Russian author Boris Pasternak best known?

3   What was the pen name of novelist Eric Blair?

4   Who illustrated Lewis Carroll's 'Alice's Adventures in Wonderland' and 'Through the Looking Glass'?

5   Who wrote 'Oranges are Not the Only Fruit' and 'Sexing the Cherry'?

6   Which American poet and humorist wrote 'You Can't Get There From Here'?

7   Which popular children's story was written by Johann Wyss?

8   What does Robinson Crusoe call the man who becomes his friend and servant in Defoe's novel?

9   Who wrote the novel 'The Thin Man'?

10 Who wrote the novels 'On the Beach' and 'A Town Like Alice'?

Entertainment

1. 'Schnozzle' was the nickname of which American entertainer?

2. What kind of creature is the cartoon character Speedy Gonzales?

3. What word was coined by Jim Henson to describe his creations which were a blend of marionettes and puppets?

4. In which country was movie star Mel Gibson born?

5. In the 'Arabian Nights' stories, what were the magic words used by Ali Baba to gain entrance to the cave of the 40 thieves?

6. Name the Belgian-born guitarist who was one of Europe's first jazz virtuosos.

7. Cartoon movie animator Walter Lantz died aged 93 in 1994. What character was his most famous creation?

8. Which American author won the 1962 Nobel Prize for Literature?

9. Which movie starring Meg Ryan and Tom Hanks was a remake of 1940's 'The Shop Around the Corner', in which James Stewart and Margaret Sullavan took the lead roles?

10. Which virtuoso alto-saxophonist was also in at the birth of bebop, collaborating with Dizzy Gillespie on such recordings as 'Ornithology' and 'Now's The Time'?

History

1   In which year was George Washington made the first president of the U.S.A.?

2   On which island did Napoleon Bonaparte die in May 1821?

3   In which year did Napoleon's Grand Army make its retreat from Moscow?

4   Which U.S. president came to office in 1977?

5   In which country did the Sharpeville Massacre happen in March 1960?

6   In which year did the Berlin Wall go up?

7   In which Caribbean country did Toussaint L'Ouverture lead a slaves' revolt from 1791 to 1794?

8   Which monarch died on the 22nd January 1901?

9   Where in the U.S.A. did the Wright brothers make their first powered flight in 1903?

10 Where was Archduke Franz Ferdinand of Austria assassinated in 1914?

General Knowledge

1 Who said about taking a course in speed reading: "I read War and Peace in ten minutes; its about Russia"?

2 Which character in 'The Arabian Nights' was the son of Mustafa the Tailor?

3 Which romantic character created by novelist Gabriel Telleg is the main character of the opera 'Don Giovanni'?

4 What in area is the largest country in Africa?

5 Which is the world's largest bay?

6 In which country is Lake Disappointment?

7 What is the more common name of the flowering plant helianthus?

8 What was the pseudonym of the French writer and philosopher Francois Marie Arouet?

9 What is the official name of New York's Sixth Avenue?

10 What is crystallomancy another name for?

Movies

1. Who starred as the brash Brooklyn housewife in the movie 'For Pete's Sake'?

2. Which actress won an Academy Award nomination for her portrayal of a teenage prostitute in the 1976 movie 'Taxi Driver'?

3. Which 1982 movie starred Eddie Murphy as a small-time crook, and Nick Nolte as a San Francisco cop?

4. Who starred as the adopted American Indian Jack Crabb in the 1970 movie 'Little Big Man'?

5. Which 1995 French movie starred Juliette Binoche and Olivier Martinez as aristocrats fleeing a cholera epidemic?

6. Which 'Twin Peaks' star played a casino entertainment boss in the 1995 movie 'Showgirls'?

7. Which director made a cameo appearance in every one of his movies from 1926's 'The Lodger' onwards?

8. Which Disney movie won a special Academy Award in 1938 for significant screen innovation?

9. Who plays Austin Powers in the movies?

10. The Julie Christie/Donald Sutherland movie 'Don't Look Now' was based on a story by which writer?

Mythology

1. What was the name of the hall in Asgard where Odin feasted with heroes killed in battle?

2. Who was the Greek god of wine?

3. Which Gorgon was so ugly that all who saw her face were turned to stone?

4. Who was the escaped slave who removed a thorn from a lion's paw in an ancient Roman story?

5. In Greek mythology, who was the wife of Orpheus who died from a snake bite?

6. According to legend, which sacred object was brought to the English town of Glastonbury by Joseph of Arimathea?

7. In Greek mythology, by which part of Achilles's body did his mother hold him when she dipped him into the river Styx?

8. According to legend, which twins were the founders of Rome?

9. Which mythical creature was part lion, part goat and part serpent?

10. Which legendary bird cremates itself and rises from its own ashes once every 500 years?

Art

1 Which British landscape painter painted 'The White Horse' and 'The Haywain'?

2 Which Italian painter and architect had the surname di Bondone?

3 Which artist and typographer carved the 'Stations of the Cross' in London's Westminster Cathedral?

4 Which well-known portrait is Sir Thomas Gainsborough's most famous work?

5 What nationality was the painter and sculptor Alberto Giacometti?

6 Which movement in painting is associated with Van Gogh, Cézanne and Gauguin?

7 Which English artist illustrated the published edition of Oscar Wilde's play 'Salome'?

8 Which pointillist artist painted 'Sunday Afternoon on the Island of La Grande Jatte'?

9 In 1975, whose painting, 'The Nightwatch', was stolen in Amsterdam by an unemployed teacher with a butcher's knife?

10 On which island was the painter El Greco born?

General Knowledge

1. Which playwright of ancient Greece wrote the comic plays 'The Wasps' 'The Birds' and 'The Frogs'?

2. Which conflict of 1982 was described as "Two bald men fighting over a comb"?

3. Boxer, Muhammad Ali (then Cassius Clay) was born in which U.S. city in 1942?

4. Mount Kailash, an imposing 22,000 feet high mountain revered in Hinduism and Buddhism as an abode of gods (and therefore it may never be climbed), is in which country?

5. Samarkand, Bukhara, Bam and Damascus are some of the cities sited on which trade route of ancient times?

6. Who was the Vietnamese communist whose leadership resulted in the country's independence from France in 1954?

7. Which Australian feminist wrote 'The Female Eunuch'?

8. Which British explorer lost his ship the 'Endurance', to the Antarctic ice in 1915, resulting in a party having to set off in a lifeboat to find rescue on South Georgia, 800 miles away?

9. Which nation was confederated in 1815, unified in 1871, federalized in 1949 and reunified in 1990?

10. The Great Barrier Reef lies at the western side of which sea?

Politics

1 Who became U.S. Secretary of Defense after Ronald Reagan's presidential victory in 1980?

2 In a 1989 event which signalled the end of the Berlin Wall, which Eastern Bloc country opened its borders to the West?

3 Which country was the first to grant all its women the right to vote?

4 Who did Sara Jane Moore attempt to assassinate in San Francisco in 1975?

5 Which country was invaded by Iraq in 1980?

6 What is the minimum age at which someone can be elected U.S. president?

7 At which battle in June 1942 was the first defeat inflicted on the Japanese navy since the 16th century?

8 Bob Woodward and Carl Bernstein, who first broke the Watergate story, were reporters with which newspaper?

9 Who was the only American president to resign the presidency?

10 Which American frontiersman and one time Member of Congress, was killed at the Alamo?

Nationalities

1 Explorer, Marco Polo was a national of which city-state?

2 Film director, Alfred Hitchcock was born in which country in 1899?

3 Born in Russia and later a French national, what was composer, Igor Stravinsky's nationality when he died in 1971?

4 In which European country was American conductor/composer Andre Previn born?

5 Former U.S. Ambassador to the United Nations, Madeleine Albright, was born in which European country?

6 What nationality is former United Nations General Secretary, Kofi Annan?

7 Former football-ace, Pele, is a national of which country?

8 In which country was astronomer, Nicolaus Copernicus born?

9 Astronomer, Tycho Brahe and explorer, Vitus Bering were both from which country?

10 In spite of his Polish name and affected Polish accent, conductor Leopold Stokowski was born in which country?

Classical Music

1. Who composed the music for the ballet 'La Boutique Fantasque'?

_____

2. Who arranged the music for 'La Boutique Fantasque'?

_____

3. Who composed the music for the ballet 'Daphnis and Chloe'?

_____

4. What is the name of the spirits of dead girls who dance at night and lure men to their destruction in 'Giselle'?

_____

5. Who composed the ballet (or 'masque for dancing' as the composer preferred to call it), entitled 'Job'?

_____

6. Which ballet by Aram Khatchaturian includes the famous 'Sabre Dance'?

_____

7. From which of Tchaikovsky's ballets does 'The Dance of the Sugar-Plum Fairy' come?

_____

8. In which ballet by Stravinsky are the central characters three puppets?

_____

9. What nationality was the composer Jean Sibelius?

_____

10. What is the common name of Beethoven's 'Piano Sonata No. 14 in C Sharp Minor'?

The Animal Kingdom

1 What is another name for the Russian wolfhound?

_____

2 What type of creature is a blind snake?

_____

3 What type of creature is a keeshund?

_____

4 A cygnet is the young of which animal?

_____

5 What creatures would you find in a formicary?

_____

6 Which is the largest seabird?

_____

7 Which is the largest land bird capable of flight?

_____

8 What type of creature is a grampus?

_____

9 Which valuable gems are formed by nacre in oysters?

_____

10 The yak is a native animal of which region of the world?

General Knowledge

1 What was the proper first name of Cory Aquino, president of the Philippines from 1986-1992?

2 Long suspected of the massacre of 22,000 Polish military officers at Katyn Forest in 1940, which country finally admitted responsibility for this crime in 1990?

3 Nobel prizewinner, Aung San Suu Kyi is a popular political figure of which Asian country?

4 Which is the only Asian country, apart from China, India and Pakistan, to hold nuclear weapons?

5 Which band released their highly successful album, 'Urban Hymns' in 1997?

6 Where in the United States did Israeli leader Menachem Begin and Egyptian leader Anwar Sadat secretly meet in 1978 in order to agree a peace treaty between them?

7 Which gas is commonly called 'marsh gas'?

8 Point Barrow, on the Arctic Ocean coast, is the northernmost point of which country?

9 Which Russian city stands at the mouth of the River Neva?

10 Which London theatre was destroyed by fire in1613, then in the 1990s reconstructed to its original design with the assistance of film actor/producer Sam Wanamaker?

Geography

1 Which place of pilgrimage in south-western France is associated with St. Bernadette?

2 Which sea lies between the Gulf of Genoa and Corsica?

3 What is the legislative capital of South Africa?

4 What is the largest hot desert in the world?

5 Which notorious face of the Eiger, in Switzerland, is one of the most difficult climbs in the Alps?

6 Which American state separates the Atlantic Ocean and the Gulf of Mexico?

7 If you travelled directly east from Cape Horn, which is the next land you would reach?

8 The Aswan Dams stand astride which river?

9 Which one of the world's rivers contains the most water?

10 What was the former name of the Indian Ocean island state of Sri Lanka?

Sport

1. Gordie Howe and Wayne Gretzky are famous names in which sport?

2. The triathlon is a sport involving running, swimming and which other discipline?

3. In December 2000, he signed a lucrative 10-year contract: in which sport is Alex Rodriguez a big name?

4. Reckoned to be the oldest trophy in international sport, it was badly damaged by a Maori protestor in New Zealand in March 1997. Which trophy?

5. What word was army slang for a raw recruit and is now used in sport, especially golf and American football, to describe a first year professional?

6. In which sport would a competitor perform a choctow?

7. Wilt Chamberlain was the first person to be paid $100,000 a season in which sport?

8. Which ball game of native North American origin is played with a stick with a net at one end?

9. At which sport did William (Bill) Tilden excel during the 1920s?

10. Which American baseball great was nicknamed 'The Georgia Peach'?

The Bible

1 During the 14th century, which scholar and reformer first translated the Bible into English?

2 Which woman demanded the head of John the Baptist?

3 In return for how many pieces of silver did Judas betray Jesus?

4 During the Israelites flight from Egypt, God punished them for worshipping which artefact?

5 In which book of the Bible does a fiery red dragon with seven heads appear?

6 What is the traditional landing place of Noah's Ark?

7 When Adam and Eve were sent from the Garden of Eden, the land was made to produce only what?

8 Whose almond-tree rod flowered and produced fruit?

9 With what did Samson 'slay the Philistines'?

10 How many were the Plagues of Egypt?

General Knowledge

1   Arcadia was an idyllic rural region of which country?

2   In which country is the city of Tangier?

3   Which are the highest type of clouds, stratocumulus or cirrus?

4   The Quetzal is the unit of currency of which Central American country?

5   What name is given to a thin sheet of wood applied to the surface of furniture made of a cheaper material?

6   Orly airport is to the south of which capital city?

7   Which is the only U.S. state that shares a border with just one other state?

8   Which male Christian name, beginning with O, is the Italian form of Roland?

9   What is the name of the tower of volcanic rock in Wyoming used as a setting for the movie 'Close Encounters of the Third Kind'?

10 In which movie did Julie Andrews play Gertrude Lawrence?

History

1. What name was given to a Japanese pilot who flew suicide missions in World War II?

2. Which Scottish surgeon was the first European to trace the course of the River Niger?

3. Which ancient city was also called Ilium?

4. Which Soviet cosmonaut was the first man in space?

5. The first department store, Marshall Field, was first opened in which American city?

6. Who, in 1888, patented the pneumatic bicycle tyre?

7. Who, in 1849, were referred to as the 'Forty-Niners'?

8. Which countries were defeated by the forces of Napoleon at the Battle of Austerlitz in 1805?

9. Of what was 'ENIAC' the first of its type?

10. What did Richard J. Gatling invent in 1862?

Crime

1 Which American gangster is thought to have been responsible for the St. Valentine's Day Massacre?

2 What form of defence in a criminal prosecution is a Latin word meaning 'elsewhere'?

3 Which infamous couple were shot dead at a police road-block in Louisiana on 23rd May 1934?

4 By what nickname was the convicted criminal Robert Stroud known?

5 In which city was John Lennon shot dead in December 1980?

6 D.A. is an abbreviation for which legal official in the U.S.?

7 What was American gangster 'Lucky' Luciano's first name?

8 Which American outlaw was killed by gang member Robert Ford for a $10,000 reward?

9 What was the nickname of American gangster George Kelly?

10 Carlton Barrett and Peter Tosh in 1987 and Junior Braithwaite in 1999 were all murdered in Jamaica. At one time or another, all three were members of which band?

Assassinations

1   What was the name of the Israeli prime minister who was shot and killed in 1995?

2   Mehmet Ali Agca failed in his attempt to assassinate which prominent figure in 1981?

3   In which U.S. city was Martin Luther King killed in 1968?

4   Which Scottish king was allegedly murdered by future king, Malcolm III, in 1057?

5   Which Egyptian president was assassinated as he attended a military parade in 1981?

6   What were the first names of the two Ghandis (mother and son); Indian prime ministers who were assassinated in 1984 and 1991 respectively?

7   John Wilkes Booth shot and killed which U.S. president in 1865?

8   King Faisal II was the last king of which country when he and numerous members of his family and court were executed in a 1958 military coup?

9   In 1979, which close associate of the British royal family was killed by an IRA bomb during a fishing trip in Ireland?

10 What nationality was diplomat Count Folke Bernadotte assassinated in Israel by Zionist extremists in 1948?

Travel and Transport

1 Which American aviator crossed the Atlantic in 'The Spirit of St Louis' in 1927?

2 What name did father and son, Malcolm and Donald Campbell, give to their vehicles in which they both set world land and water speed records?

3 On 17 November 1913, the steamship 'Louise' became the first ship to pass through which canal?

4 In September 1967, which European country switched from driving on the left of the road to driving on the right?

5 In 1908, the American car firms Buick and Oldsmobile merged to form which company?

6 Which British aviators made the first nonstop flight across the Atlantic in 1919?

7 What nationality was Ernst Mach, the physicist after whom Mach numbers were named?

8 The first jet passenger aircraft to be constructed with engines at the rear of the fuselage rather than on the wings was French. What was its name?

9 In 1933 which American aviator made the first solo flight around the world?

10 Which motor car manufacturer was founded by Giovanni Agnelli in Turin in 1899?

General Knowledge

1 What is Austria's official language?

2 Which branch of the United States military became a separate entity in September 1947?

3 Near to which German city is the site of the first Nazi concentration camp, Dachau?

4 Who created the Muppets in 1955?

5 Which civilisation was centred on Mexico's Yucatan peninsula from around 2000 B.C. to the 17th century?

6 Which art term describes Western designs based on Chinese ornamental art?

7 What kind of naval vessels were the Japanese ships Hiryu, Soryu and Akagi; all of them sunk in World War II?

8 Which Indian city was renamed Chennai in the 1990s?

9 Which is the northernmost of the contiguous states of the U.S.A.? (i.e. Alaska and Hawaii excluded).

10 Having moved from acting to politics, who became known as 'The Governator' and 'Conan the Republican'?

Pop Music

1 Which group issued 'Alive in America' in 1995?

2 Which group sent 'Good News From the Next World'?

3 In 1994 '30 Years of Maximum R&B' came out for ___?

4 During 1994 George Michael released his album ___?

5 In 1983 Michael Jackson produced the album which set the standard by which all albums since have been judged. It was called ___?

6 1993 produced 'Promises and Lies' by ___?

7 In 1998 Madonna shone again, with ___?

8 'Down Under' was an album which did rather well for ___?

9 At eight minutes plus, which single in 1971 became one of the longest-ever songs to hit the pop charts?

10 Which rock group was formed in 1967 by Ian Anderson and Glenn Cornick?

The Human Body

1 Which bone in the human body is the one that is most frequently broken?

2 In which part of the human body are the metacarpals?

3 Which organ of the body is inflamed in a case of hepatitis?

4 In medicine, what is the most widespread parasitic infection?

5 In which part of the human body is the Organ of Corti?

6 Which disease is caused by a deficiency of vitamin B1 or thiamine?

7 Which organ of the human body produces and secretes bile?

8 Which common adolescent skin complaint is caused by inflammation of the sebaceous glands?

9 Which contagious disease is also called infectious parotitis?

10 Which organ that develops in pregnant women provides the unborn baby with nourishment and oxygen?

Movies

1 Which 1995 movie starred Kevin Bacon as a convict and Christian Slater as his defense attorney?

2 Who directed and starred in 1985's 'Pale Rider'?

3 'Home Improvement' star Tim Allen played a toy salesman in which 1994 Christmas movie?

4 The attempted assassination of which pop artist and movie-maker was the subject of a 1996 movie by Mary Harron?

5 Who won a Best Supporting Actress Oscar in 1984 for her performance in 'A Passage to India'?

6 Which 1995 political comedy movie was directed by 'When Harry Met Sally' director Rob Reiner?

7 Which half-Russian actor played a conniving gladiator ring operator in the 1960 movie 'Spartacus'?

8 Who starred as Rusty Sabich in the 1990 movie 'Presumed Innocent'?

9 Who directed 'The Keystone Cops' movie series?

10 Which famous cowboy character was played by Clayton Moore?

General Knowledge

1. Planes of which two airlines were involved in the 9/11 attacks on the World Trade Center twin towers?

2. Author of 'Das Kapital', which German-born political theorist was buried at London's Highgate cemetery in 1883?

3. Which well-known theatre district derives its name from the Dutch term 'Breede Weg'?

4. Which retail brand was introduced by Swede, Ingvar Kamprad?

5. Who is/was the wife of Rupert Murdoch against whom the media magnate began divorce proceedings in 2013?

6. The German army defeated which other country at the 1914 Battle of Tannenberg?

7. Ferdinand Joseph Lamothe was the real name of which jazz pianist?

8. Spider, hermit and fiddler are species of which crustacean?

9. Venice's international airport is named after which explorer?

10. The name of which musical instrument has its origins in the Greek word, 'kithara'?

Literature

1 Which Irish dramatist wrote 'Waiting for Godot'?

2 Who was the most famous creation of the Australian author P. L. Travers?

3 Which Irish author wrote 'The Old Boys' and 'The Ballroom of Romance'?

4 Which English poet is best known for nautical ballads such as 'Drake's Drum'?

5 Which Roman poet is known for his '16 Satires'?

6 Who wrote the novel 'Fair Stood the Wind for France'?

7 Which novel by Margaret Mitchell won the Pulitzer Prize for fiction in 1937?

8 Which epic poem attributed to Homer describes Odysseus' journey home after the Trojan War?

9 What was the sequel to Anita Loos' book 'Gentlemen Prefer Blondes'?

10 What was the sequel to 'Alice in Wonderland' called?

Food and Drink

1 Goulash is a traditional stew in which country?

2 The pods of which plant, also called lady's fingers, are used to make gumbo?

3 Which country is the world's largest producer of coffee?

4 Which fruit is a cross between an orange and a tangerine?

5 Which dish, consisting of chicken, peas and carrots in a white sauce was created by Thomas Jefferson, 3rd U.S. president?

6 What R is the active form of vitamin A found in margarines, oily fish and dairy fats?

7 Which stimulant is found in coffee, tea and kola nuts?

8 Which French city and wine centre on the river Garonne is the capital of the Gironde department?

9 What is the fruit of the plant citrus aurantum?

10 Which sweet, syrupy, organic liquid is the basis of all fats and oils, and is also used in the manufacture of explosives?

Shakespeare

1   Which character says: "Yet I do fear thy nature; It is too full o' the milk of human kindness."?

2   According to the title of a Shakespeare play, what city is Timon from?

3   What were the surnames of Romeo and Juliet?

4   In 'The Merchant of Venice', who would not have given "a ring for a wilderness of monkeys"?

5   Which king of Scotland, subject of a Shakespeare play, killed Duncan I?

6   Which play features Prospero, Miranda and Caliban?

7   In 'A Midsummer Night's Dream', who is the Queen of the Fairies?

8   Which play opens with the words: "If music be the food of love, play on"?

9   In which play does Duke Vincentio disguise himself as a friar?

10 What was the name of Othello's wife?

History

1. With which branch of social science was Bronislaw Malinowski associated?

2. Which former U.S. First Lady helped to found a treatment clinic for addiction?

3. Which ancient symbol was adopted by the Nazis in Germany as their emblem?

4. Which newspaper editor's escape from South Africa was featured in the movie 'Cry Freedom'?

5. What was the nickname of the American frontierswoman born Martha Jane Canary?

6. Which German field marshal was known as the Desert Fox?

7. Which astronaut hit the first golf ball on the Moon?

8. Which of the Seven Wonders of the Ancient World was built by King Nebuchadnezzar for his wife?

9. What nationality was explorer Ferdinand Magellan?

10. What, in 1926, did 'Variety' magazine describe as "a new development in radio."?

General Knowledge

1. In 1888, who was the first person to market a camera simple enough for an amateur to operate?

2. What name is given to a line on a weather map joining places of equal atmospheric pressure?

3. In what type of auction is the price progressively lowered until a buyer accepts?

4. What is the capital of the Canadian province of Nova Scotia?

5. What is the common nickname of Dvorak's 'Symphony No. 9'?

6. Which of the tropics lies immediately to the north of Cuba; Cancer or Capricorn?

7. Found in the Premier Diamond Mine in Transvaal in 1905, what is the name of the largest diamond ever found?

8. Whose law states that "Work expands so as to fill the time available for its completion."?

9. Of what is 'triskaidekaphobia' the fear?

10. What is the largest city in Switzerland?

Sport

1 At the 1968 Olympics, what did Tommie Smith and John Carlos do which brought both indignation and praise?

2 Which U.S. female tennis player, winner of nine Grand Slam titles, had to retire at age 19 after a riding accident in 1954?

3 Where in Belgium is the country's main Formula One racing circuit?

4 Brother and sister former world ski champions, Andreas and Hanni Wenzel, come from which country?

5 In which year of the 20th century did Tokyo host the Summer Olympic Games?

6 For which U.S. soccer team did Pele play for from 1975-1977?

7 What was the surname of father and son Italian racing drivers Antonio and Alberto, both killed at age 36, on the race track in 1925 and 1955?

8 Which golfer lost the 1991 Ryder Cup on the final putt?

9 The Formula One Drivers' Championship was inaugurated in 1950; where was the first race?

10 Why was Muhammad Ali stripped of his World Heavyweight boxing title in 1967?

War

1 In which country was the Nazi war criminal Adolf Eichmann seized by Israeli agents in 1960?

_____

2 Which American physicist was put in charge of the development of the atom bomb at Los Alamos in 1943?

_____

3 In which village in South Vietnam were civilians massacred by American soldiers in March 1968?

_____

4 Which European country held Beirut from World War I until it became capital of the newly-independent Lebanon?

_____

5 Who, during the Vietnam War, was known as 'Hanoi Jane'?

_____

6 What code name was used by the U.S. for the project from 1942 which developed the atomic bomb?

_____

7 Which 1999 World War II movie set in the Pacific featured Sean Penn, George Clooney, Nick Nolte and Woody Harrelson?

_____

8 What D is a minstrel song which became the battle hymn of the confederacy during the American Civil War?

_____

9 In which German city were the trials of the main Nazi war criminals held after World War II?

_____

10 Which relief agency was founded in 1864 to assist the wounded in wars?

ROUND 201

Science

1 What is the name of the largest asteroid and the first to be discovered?

_____

2 Which scientist famously used kites to conduct experiments on atmospheric electrical phenomena?

_____

3 What is the more common name of diluted acetic acid?

_____

4 What name is given to a place equipped with telescopes for studying the sky?

_____

5 Which building material is mixed with water and materials such as sand and crushed stone to make concrete?

_____

6 What name is given to the scientific study or exploration of caves?

_____

7 What name is given to a device that measures atmospheric pressure?

_____

8 Which English scientist discovered the principle of electromagnetic induction in 1831?

_____

9 Which form of partly dehydrated gypsum is used for making casts and moulds?

_____

10 What name is given to the shaping of something so that it meets the least resistance when travelling through water or air?

General Knowledge

1 Beethoven, Schubert, Bruckner, Dvorak, Mahler and Vaughan Williams all composed the same number of symphonies: how many?

2 The tile of which novel by John Steinbeck is a four-word phrase contained in a poem by Robert Burns?

3 'A Passage to India' of 1984, was the last film of which director?

4 'Lord of the Rings' author, J.R.R. Tolkien was born in which country?

5 Which seabird gets its name from the historical belief that its presence preceded bad weather?

6 Which Greek island was the home of the poet Sappho?

7 In Islamic countries, what is the title of an official who summons people to pray five times a day?

8 In the NATO phonetic alphabet, the name of which capital city represents letter 'L'?

9 Which French two-word expression, meaning 'false step' has been adopted in English as a term for a mistake or blunder?

10 Which word connects a small breed of chicken and a weight category in the sport of boxing?

Geography

1. Which U.S. state comprises the former Sandwich Islands?

2. Which mountain chain forms a natural barrier between France and Spain?

3. Which arm of the Mediterranean Sea lies between Greece and Turkey?

4. Amsterdam is the largest city in the Netherlands; which is the second-largest?

5. The Mozambique Channel separates which island from mainland Africa?

6. Which seventeenth century Dutch explorer discovered New Zealand?

7. Which continent has the longest coastline?

8. Which major sea is so shallow that it has no tides?

9. Which island in the Indian Ocean was described by Mark Twain as the "prototype of heaven"?

10. On which river in North America are the Horseshoe Falls?

Jazz

1. Who was the 'Prince of Darkness' who gave us 'cool' jazz?

---

2. Who led what is considered today to have been the first 'real' jazz band?

---

3. Who was the Kansas city based pianist and leader of big band 'swing' who composed 'One O'clock Jump'?

---

4. Which other great jazz 'original' persuaded Louis Armstrong to give up the cornet and concentrate on the trumpet?

---

5. Freddie Keppard was one of New Orlean's leading jazz trumpet players. What was his nickname?

---

6. Which New Orleans-born saxophonist and clarinettist began his career with Freddie Keppard's band at only eight years of age? He died in France in 1959.

---

7. Who was the trumpeter and band-leader renowned for improvization, especially with 'Dippermouth Blues'?

---

8. Who, with his 'Red Hot Peppers' made the best recordings ever of New Orleans music in the 1920s?

---

9. What instrument was played by jazz great Artie Shaw?

---

10. In which 1999 Woody Allen movie did Sean Penn play fictitious Thirties jazz guitarist Emmet Ray?

Around the Islands

1. Two countries share the Caribbean island of Hispaniola: one is the Dominican Republic, what is the other?

2. Which tiny island, part of the U.K., lies 300 miles west of Scotland and gives its name to a sea area?

3. Which European country holds sovereignty over Greenland?

4. The Atlantic island group, the Azores, belong to which country?

5. The Bahamas lie to the east of which U.S. state?

6. The Croatian islands of Hvar and Korcula lie in which sea?

7. Which is the largest island in the Caribbean Sea?

8. The Svalbard island group in the Arctic Ocean, belongs to which European country?

9. The Aleutian islands belong to which U.S. state?

10. Which Portuguese island is located about 360 miles off the western coast of Morocco?

Space

1. The asteroid belt lies between which two planets of the solar system?

2. Titan, Mimas, Rhea and Dione are just four of the 20 known moons of which planet?

3. What from Earth is eclipsed when the Moon moves between Earth and the Sun?

4. In which U.S. state is the Keek telescope, which in 1995 located the most distant galaxy up until then discovered (some 15 billion light years away)?

5. Betelgeuse is one of the brightest stars in which constellation?

6. The stars Castor and Pollux are in which constellation of the night sky?

7. At the age of 77, who became America's oldest astronaut?

8. What first was achieved by Sally Ride in 1983?

9. What was the name of the first space station?

10. Which group of stars in the night sky represents a hunter with belt and sword?

General Knowledge

1   On which Atlantic island group is the dormant volcano, Mount Teide?

_____

2   Which popular toy was called the Pluto Platter when it first appeared in 1955?

_____

3   Alexander Dubcek was the leader of which country when it was invaded by Soviet forces in 1968?

_____

4   An expedition led by Englishman, Sir Vivian Fuchs achieved which feat in 1958?

_____

5   Where on birds (and certain other animal) are its nictitating membranes?

_____

6   The comet of 44 B.C. is named after which emperor, who died in that year?

_____

7   Which North America animal, which probably numbered sixty million in the 18th century, was, due to hunting, almost brought to the point of extinction by 1900?

_____

8   Scene of a long siege by Saladin's forces in 1183-84, Kerak Castle is in which present-day country?

_____

9   In Norse mythology, which god is called the 'Allfather'?

_____

10   In which South America country is the extensive upland region of Mato Grosso?

Religion

1. Which term, meaning 'lord' in certain Middle Eastern languages, applies to a number of Bronze Age deities worshipped in that region?

2. Which modern-day Asian religion has its roots in Brahmanism?

3. Of the world's religions, which has the greatest number of followers?

4. ISKCON is the abbreviation of the title of the religious movement known generally as what?

5. In 1997, thirty-nine members of which American religious cult group were found dead in San Diego, having committed mass suicide?

6. The Kitabi-i-Iqan, The Book of Certitude, is a collection of works belonging to which religion?

7. The Islamic Calendar has its first year as that of the journey of Muhammad from Mecca to which other sacred city?

8. In Judaism, what is the name of the small boxes worn by rabbi's during ceremonies?

9. What is the sacred river of the Hindu religion?

10. The Falashas are a Jewish people who live in which East African country?

History

1. Which American general famously pledged "I shall return"?

2. Which Siberian peasant and mystic exerted harmful influence over Nicholas II of Russia?

3. What was the first name of the ballet dancer Nijinsky?

4. Of which French king was Madame Du Barry a mistress?

5. Which Roman highway was named after Appius Claudius Caecus?

6. What name was given to the bubonic plague epidemic that ravaged Europe in the 14th century?

7. Which reclusive American tycoon designed the wooden flying boat known as the 'Spruce Goose'?

8. After which Italian navigator was America named?

9. What was the name of the Roman practise of killing every tenth man in a cowardly or mutinous military unit?

10. Which French king, who reigned from 1643-1715, professed to hold his power from God and is supposed to have said: "L'etat c'est moi" (I am the State)?

Poetry

1 Which American poet wrote 'A Road Not Taken' and 'Fire and Ice'?

2 How many sonnets comprise the famous collection written by Shakespeare?

3 'Don Juan', written in 1818, is probably the most popular work of which poet?

4 Which poem by Edward Lear concerns the relationship between an avian and a feline?

5 Born in Horsham, England, which poet drowned, aged 29 off the coast of Tuscany in 1822?

6 Complete the title of the poem by Anna Akhmatova: 'A Poem Without a ...'?

7 Which poem by John Masefield begins 'I must go down to the seas again'?

8 'On the Road' by Jack Kerouac and Alan Ginsberg's 'Howl' are poems are two examples of what style of 1950s poetry?

9 Which poem by William Blake, set to music by Hubert Parry, has become Britain's "second national anthem"?

10 'Nevermore' appears several times, and is the last word in which of Edgar Allan Poe's poems?

General Knowledge

1 The Diet is the name of the government of which country?

2 In which country is Hamelin, home of the Pied Piper of legend?

3 Which English writer and physician wrote 'Studies in the Psychology of Sex'?

4 What is the most westerly capital city of mainland Europe?

5 According to tradition, rain will fall for forty days and nights if it rains on which saint's feast day?

6 How are the Malvinas Islands better known?

7 Which landlocked country has the in Gobi Desert in the south and east and the Altai Mountains in the west?

8 Josiah Warren, who stated that "Every man should be his own government, own law, own church" is said to be the first American practitioner of which philosophy?

9 Ariel is the spirit who must serve the magician Prospero, in which of Shakespeare's plays?

10 In which European capital city is the medical university, the Karolinska Institute?

Entertainment

1. The principal symphony orchestra of which German city was Herbert von Karajan musical director from 1955 to 1989?

2. Which songwriter wrote 'Over the Rainbow' for Judy Garland?

3. Lord Greystoke was the father of which fictional character of book and movie fame?

4. Which actor's biography was entitled 'My Wicked, Wicked Ways'?

5. Which composer's famous last words were purported to be: 'I shall hear in heaven.'?

6. What type of dog is Snoopy in the cartoon strip 'Peanuts'?

7. In the 'Peanuts' cartoon strip, what kind of creature is Woodstock?

8. What relation is Whitney Houston to Dionne Warwick?

9. The symphony orchestra of which American city did George Szell conduct from 1946 until his death in 1970?

10. What were the names of the opposing gangs in the musical 'West Side Story'?

Nature

1 Which tree's leaves and bark do koala bears feed on?

_____

2 Which insect transmits sleeping sickness to humans?

_____

3 Which is bigger, the African elephant or the Indian elephant?

_____

4 Which parasitic fungus affects cereal grasses such as rye and can cause gangrene in humans?

_____

5 By what name is the tree Cedrus libani better known?

_____

6 Which branch of biology deals with the study of animals?

_____

7 Which marine crustacean has a front pair of legs modified as pincers, one for crushing and one for cutting?

_____

8 A leveret is the young of which creature?

_____

9 What creature was once called a camelopard because it resembled a cross between a camel and a leopard?

_____

10 In which country is the black swan found?

Mythology

1 On which vessel did Jason and the Argonauts sail in search of the Golden Fleece?

_____

2 In mythology, who is the Norse God of Thunder?

_____

3 In Greek mythology, which youth fell in love with his own reflection in a pool?

_____

4 As one of his labours, what task did Hercules have to do with the 'Cretan bull'?

_____

5 Who were the one-eyed giants of Greek mythology?

_____

6 Which is the only planet that is not named after a god of classical mythology?

_____

7 In mythology, the wife of Odin gave her name to which day of the week?

_____

8 Who was the Roman goddess of the dawn?

_____

9 Which mythological animal had the body and head of a woman and the feet and wings of a vulture?

_____

10 Who in mythology rode a horse called Xanthus?

Movies

1. Which 'Star Trek' character was played on television and in movies by DeForest Kelley?

_____

2. Who directed the 1977 movie 'New York New York'?

_____

3. Which 'Four Weddings and a Funeral' actress starred in the 1995 movie 'Unstrung Heroes'?

_____

4. What was the name of Audrey Hepburn's character in the 1961 movie 'Breakfast at Tiffany's'?

_____

5. Which controversial former American football star played Nordberg in 'The Naked Gun' movies?

_____

6. Which low-budget movie about three Catholic brothers won the top prize at America's Sundance Film Festival in 1995?

_____

7. Who played Isaac Davis in the 1979 movie 'Manhattan'?

_____

8. What is the name of Humphrey Bogart's character in 'The Maltese Falcon'?

_____

9. In which movie does Doris Day sing 'Secret Love'?

_____

10. In the 1960s, Anette Funicello starred in a series of beach movies with which actor/singer?

General Knowledge

1   Which famous novel was written in 1924 by Percival Christopher Wren, an ex-member of the French Foreign Legion?

_____

2   Which cold dry northerly wind is funnelled down the Rhône Valley to the Mediterranean?

_____

3   What would be cultivated in an arboretum?

_____

4   What name is given to the study of human populations?

_____

5   Which nurse was nicknamed 'The Lady with the Lamp' by her patients?

_____

6   What was the first capital of the U.S.A. from 1789 to 1790?

_____

7   Which fabric is named after the Iraqi city of Mosul?

_____

8   Which fabric used for jeans takes its name from the French city of Nimes?

_____

9   The Elgin Marbles, now in the British Museum, were originally taken from which Greek building?

_____

10   What is the third colour of the rainbow?

Music

1. Which popular female country and western singer was killed in a plane crash in March 1963?

2. What was the country of birth of Sergei Rachmaninov, the composer, pianist and conductor, 1873-1943?

3. Who was popularly considered to have been the greatest guitar virtuoso of all time?

4. Which of the three Strauss brothers composed the famous waltz 'Village Swallows'?

5. Which of the three Strauss brothers composed the famous waltz 'The Blue Danube'?

6. The composer, Mozart was born in which Austrian city in 1756?

7. In 1979, which group put out 'Cool For Cats'?

8. Who was 'Born to Run' in 1975?

9. Who is the English-born alto-saxophonist, band leader and composer of all kinds of jazz, including 'Experiments With Mice', 'African Waltz' and many movie scores?

10. Which pianist and bandleader died in Kansas City at only 39 years of age? A charismatic singer of his own songs such as 'Honeysuckle Rose', his left hand was so powerful that a rhythm section was almost superfluous.

Sport

1 In a game of football, what is the distance between the two goal posts?

2 Where are the headquarters of the United States of America Cricket Association, the governing body formed in 1965?

3 Due to security threats in Mauritania, which led to the cancellation of the 2008 rally, the Dakar Rally (formerly the Paris-Dakar Rally) has run in which continent since 2009?

4 In 2013, which team won Super Bowl XLVII after beating the San Francisco 49ers 34-31?

5 Italian ex-Formula 1 driver Alessandro Zanardi, who lost both legs following a crash in 2001, won two Paralympic golds in 2012 in which sport?

6 In the 2012 Paralympics, Nazmiye Muslu won in the -40kg powerlifting category, giving which country its only gold medal?

7 How many members of a basketball team can be actively playing on the court at any one time?

8 Steph Gilmore, Kelly Slater, Layne Beachley and Mick Fanning have all become world champions in which sport?

9 The Mongol Rally is a car rally that begins in Europe and ends in which capital city?

10 Which stadium is home to Mass United F.C., an American soccer team based in Lynn, Massachusetts?

Literature

1. Which French author wrote the novel 'Madame Bovary'?

_____

2. In John Milton's 'Paradise Lost', which fallen angel is ranked second to Satan in power?

_____

3. Who wrote the novels 'Rich Man, Poor Man' and 'Beggarman, Thief'?

_____

4. Which Norwegian dramatist wrote 'Hedda Gabler'?

_____

5. Which English writer was best known for his translation of the 'Rubaiyat of Omar Khayyam'?

_____

6. How many lines are there in a sonnet?

_____

7. Which well-known horror story was written by Mary Shelley?

_____

8. Which American author wrote 'I Know Why The Caged Bird Sings'?

_____

9. The character of The Mad Hatter in 'Alice in Wonderland' is said to be patterned after which British prime minister?

_____

10. The action of John Le Carré's book 'A Small Town in Germany' takes place in which small town?

General Knowledge

1. Which empire ruled Egypt at the time of the birth of Jesus?

2. Causing the deaths of at least 25 million people, what was the deadliest natural disaster of the 20th century?

3. Which Art Garfunkel song appeared in the film 'Watership Down'?

4. "A thing of beauty is a joy forever", a line from the poem 'Endymion', is by which poet?

5. Duane Eddy was an expert player of which instrument?

6. Which word is used to describe the brightness of stars?

7. Used in the Stone Age to tip spears and arrows, which rock has the appearance of dark bottle-glass?

8. Etymology is the study of the origins of what?

9. Frenchman, Ferdinand Lesseps is best known for what two (similar) civil engineering feats?

10. Which English cheese is the favourite of animation duo Wallace and Gromit?

History

1. Who invented the telephone in 1876?

2. Which British general was killed at the capture of Khartoum in January 1885?

3. Which present-day Asian city-state was founded by Stamford Raffles in 1819?

4. Composer, Richard Wagner was born in 1813, the same year as which famous Italian opera composer?

5. Which British general surrendered to American forces at Yorktown in 1781?

6. 5th March 1953 saw the death of which world leader?

7. Which U.S. city was damaged in an earthquake on 1st October 1987?

8. In 1985, who succeeded Chernenko to become General Secretary of the Communist Party of the U.S.S.R.?

9. In 1878, Swan and Edison, separately, invented which everyday item?

10. Which wife did Nelson Mandela divorce in March 1996?

Geography

1. Which Canadian city is the capital of Ontario?

_____

2. Which country takes its name from the Latin word for 'southern'?

_____

3. Of which country was Milton Obote the president from 1966 to 1971 and from 1980 to 1985?

_____

4. What is the highest altitude navigable lake in the world?

_____

5. What is the largest city in the American state of New Mexico?

_____

6. What is Pakistan's largest city and chief port?

_____

7. Which European country was ruled by Janos Kadar from 1956?

_____

8. Of which former Soviet state is Tallinn the capital?

_____

9. Which South American country is named after the Italian city of Venice?

_____

10. Cape Verde is the most westerly point of which continent?

The Answer's a Country

1 Which African country was formerly known as the French Territory of the Afars and Issas?

_____

2 Apart from America, which is the only other country in the world to which alligators are native?

_____

3 Nyasaland is the former name of which African republic?

_____

4 From which country did the United States make the Louisiana Purchase?

_____

5 Which country was originally called Staten Land when it was discovered in the 17th century?

_____

6 What is the second largest country in South America?

_____

7 In the 19th century, Paul Kruger was president of which country?

_____

8 In which Eastern European country would you find the town of Ploesti and the port of Constantsa?

_____

9 The port of Agadir is in which North African country?

_____

10 Of which country is Amman the capital?

U.S. Presidents

1. Apart from Ford and Bush (twice), can you name the other two U.S. presidents whose names only consisted of four letters?

2. The 10th President of the U.S.A. was the first to get married in office. Can you name him?

3. 'Where's the Rest of Me' is the autobiography of which U.S. president?

4. Who was the first U.S. vice president to succeed to the presidency?

5. Which American president was assassinated by John Wilkes Booth?

6. Who was the 15th U.S. president and the only one who never married?

7. Whom did George Bush defeat to become U.S. President in 1988?

8. Peter Hurd painted the official portrait of which American President, who remarked when it was unveiled in January 1967, that it was the ugliest thing he ever saw?

9. Which U.S. president ordered the dropping of the first atomic bomb?

10. Which future U.S. president was born in a small log cabin in Kentucky in 1809?

General Knowledge

1 Which 18th-19th century German physician gives his name to a form of hypnotism?

2 The galvanisation of metal, a process designed to prevent rusting, involves coating the base metal with which other metal?

3 Which city stands at the western terminus of the Canadian Pacific Railway?

4 Cassiterite is the most important ore in the production of which common metal?

5 Who was the Roman goddess of the dawn?

6 The title of which Joseph Heller novel, set in World War II, has come into everyday use to describe a no-win situation?

7 Later completed by Franz Süssmayr, which choral and orchestral work did Mozart leave unfinished when he died?

8 Who composed the march 'Stars and Stripes Forever'?

9 In zoology, what term describes a tail or limb which is capable of grasping?

10 Utah, Omaha, Sword, Juno and Gold relate to which major event of World War II?

Science

1 What name is given to the pumping of fuel in the form of a spray directly into the cylinders of an internal-combustion engine?

_____

2 What name is given to radioactive particles deposited from the atmosphere after a nuclear explosion?

_____

3 At which American power plant did a nuclear accident occur in 1979?

_____

4 Which two layers of the Earth's atmosphere are separated by the tropopause?

_____

5 What plant is the original source of the heart drug digitalis?

_____

6 What name is given to the hydrated crystalline form of sodium carbonate?

_____

7 Which optical toy using multiple reflections to create patterns was invented by Sir David Brewster?

_____

8 What name is given to the property of a body that causes it to remain at rest or in uniform motion until external force is applied?

_____

9 Which crystalline solid is responsible for the characteristic smell of the mint plant?

_____

10 What name is given to the series of radioactive elements with atomic numbers from 89 to 103?

_____

Politics

1 What was ended by the 13th Amendment to the U.S. Constitution?

_____

2 What did the initials U.S.S.R., describing the country of Russia and surrounding states, stand for?

_____

3 Which Mongol ruler of Samarkand sacked Delhi in 1398?

_____

4 Which former Indian prime minister was assassinated in 1991?

_____

5 Who was elected vice president of the United States in 1992?

_____

6 Which U.S. President authorized the use of the atom bomb against Japan?

_____

7 David Ben Gurion was the first prime minister of which country?

_____

8 Sir John A. MacDonald was the first prime minister of which country?

_____

9 What did Winston Churchill refer to as "a riddle wrapped in a mystery inside an enigma."?

_____

10 Whose was the briefest U.S. presidency?

Television

1 Peter Funt was the originator of which television programme; versions of which have had successful runs in both North America and the U.K.?

_____

2 What was the name of Mary Francis Crosby's character who shot J.R. in 'Dallas'?

_____

3 Which TV family lived on The Ponderosa?

_____

4 Which 'Dallas' actor played Capt. Tony Nelson in 'I Dream of Jeannie'?

_____

5 Who played Norm Paterson in 'Cheers'?

_____

6 In 'The Simpsons', who is headmaster at Bart and Lisa's school?

_____

7 Which vintage TV comedy series was set at Fort Baxter?

_____

8 In the TV series, who plays Buffy the Vampire Slayer?

_____

9 Who played Maddie Hayes in the TV series 'Moonlighting'?

_____

10 The character Fallon appeared in 'Dynasty' and which other TV series?

General Knowledge

1   King Charles, Cavalier King Charles and English Springer are all types of which breed of dog?

2   Fidelity, Bravery, Integrity is the motto of which American organization?

3   Which pistol that fires a coloured flare for signalling purposes was named after a U.S. naval ordnance officer?

4   Who wrote the popular children's book 'Heidi'?

5   What type of animal is a Lipizzaner?

6   Which word for the act of killing someone painlessly, especially to relieve suffering, is derived from the Greek for 'easy death'?

7   Carmine is a vivid shade of which colour?

8   What type of buildings did Don Quixote mistake for evil giants?

9   Originating in the U.S.A., what word means a payment awarded to a non-married partner after the break-up of a long term relationship?

10 Which carnivorous mammal has striped, spotted and brown varieties?

Classical Music

1 In which of Tchaikovsky's ballets do we meet the villainous magician Von Rothbart?

2 What is the name of the ballet choreographed by Fokine to a number of piano compositions by Chopin?

3 Stravinsky's most famous ballet scores ('Firebird', 'Petrouchka' and 'Rite of Spring') were commissioned by which great leader of the Russian ballet?

4 Who composed the ballet which became a vehicle for the superb talents of Fonteyn and Nureyev: 'Romeo and Juliet'?

5 Who was the Russian dancer considered to be the greatest of all prima ballerinas?

6 Who was called 'the god of the dance'?

7 What is a 'couplet'?

8 What is a 'fanfare'?

9 What nationality was the composer Alexander Borodin?

10 At the age of 22, Beethoven noted in his diary that he had enough money for his first music lesson with which fellow composer?

The Answer's a Number

1 How many 'Pillars of Wisdom' appear in the title of the autobiographical account of the experiences of British soldier T. E. Lawrence (aka Lawrence of Arabia)?

2 How many states of the U.S.A. begin with the letter C?

3 In the famous song from Meredith Wilson's hit 1957 Broadway musical 'The Music Man', how many trombones led the big parade?

4 What year is connected with the festival overture, Opus 49 by Russian composer Pyotr Ilyich Tchaikovsky that tells the story of Napoleon's retreat from Russia?

5 What is the square root of 9801?

6 How many leagues under the sea are in the title of the classic science fiction novel by French writer Jules Verne?

7 In Greek mythology, what was the number of labours performed by Hercules?

8 If the letters A to Z are, in order, given the numbers one to 26, what number is obtained by multiplying K by Q?

9 Given that each has the normal number of legs, how many legs have eight chickens, six sheep and four spiders?

10 DNA molecules are packaged into chromosomes. How many pairs of chromosomes has the human body?

Rulers and Leaders

1 Who succeeded Warren G. Harding as the president of the United States in 1923?

2 What title used by German emperors derives from the Latin word Caesar?

3 Who was the autocratic director-general of New Netherland who surrendered the colony to British forces in 1664?

4 Of which country was Henry Pu-Yi the last emperor?

5 Enver Hoxha was leader of which country from 1946 to 1985?

6 What nationality is former U.N. secretary-general, Javier Perez de Cuellar?

7 Born in Scotland, who was Canada's first prime minister?

8 What was Adolf Hitler's original family name?

9 Who became president of Iraq in 1979?

10 What name was adopted by Goldie Myerson when she became Israel's foreign minister in 1956?

History

1. Which Maltese-born psychologist originated the term 'lateral thinking'?

2. Which extinct early Stone Age man is represented by skeletal remains found in China?

3. In which year was the construction of the Eiffel Tower completed?

4. In 1666, what disaster originated in a bakery in Pudding Lane, London?

5. Whom did Mrs Anna Anderson claim to be from 1920 until her death in 1984?

6. To what, in 1847, did the Californian town of Yerba Buena change its name?

7. Who was the first female singer to be inducted into America's Rock and Roll Hall of Fame?

8. Which British Lord opened the tomb of Tutankhamen in November 1922?

9. In which city was the world's first underground train service opened in 1863?

10. How did Sue Rosenkawitz achieve fame in Cape Town on 11 January 1974?

General Knowledge

1. 'We Have All the Time in the World', the theme song used in the James Bond film 'On Her Majesty's Secret Service' was sung by which artist?

2. The poetry collections 'Death of a Naturalist' and 'Human Chain' were among the works of which Irish poet?

3. What natural materials do xylologists study?

4. The phrase "Tilting at Windmills" i.e. fighting imagined rivals, comes from an adventure of which mythical knight?

5. Which country is the location of the annual Nedbank Golf Challenge at Sun City?

6. Which French artist produced many works based on biblical subjects, and illustrated books by Edgar Allan Poe, Dante, Milton and Tennyson?

7. The Americas are named after which Italian explorer?

8. Which flightless bird lays the largest egg of all avians?

9. What colour is 'Eau de Nil'?

10. Which famous airship caught fire and crashed at Lakehurst, New Jersey in 1937?

Movies

1. Until the success of 'Titanic' at the 1998 Academy Awards, which movie held the record for winning the most Oscars?

2. Who is the only person to have been nominated for an Oscar as producer, director, actor and screenwriter in the same year?

3. Which outlaw was played by Robert Redford in the 1969 movie 'Butch Cassidy and the Sundance Kid'?

4. Which Stanley Kubrick movie was based on a Stephen King novel and starred Jack Nicholson?

5. Which 1999 'Star Trek' send-up starred Sigourney Weaver as blonde communications officer Lieutenant Tawny Madison?

6. Which 2000 horror sequel saw Courteney Cox Arquette reprising her role as a television reporter and her husband David Arquette his as a small town cop?

7. Which actor played an FBI agent investigating a death in a rundown LA hotel in the 2000 movie 'The Million Dollar Hotel'?

8. Which 1977 movie starred Henry Winkler and Sally Field as a young couple dealing with the emotional aftermath of the Vietnam War?

9. Who played the part of 'juror No. 8' in the movie '12 Angry Men'?

10. What in America was the original name for a cinema?

Religion

1. The Granth is the holy book of which religion?

2. The Notre Dame cathedral in Paris, France, is an example of what style of architecture?

3. Which novel was ceremoniously burnt by a thousand Muslims in 1989?

4. What, in Buddhism, is the sum of a person's actions in previous existences?

5. The statue Christ of the Andes stands on the border between Argentina and which other country?

6. Who founded the Society of Friends, also known as the Quakers?

7. Which Christian sect is named after Dutch Anabaptist leader Menno Simons?

8. What is the name of the famous onion-domed cathedral in Red Square, Moscow?

9. Which Cistercian order of monks are noted for their austerity and vow of silence?

10. Which Gothic Paris cathedral is famous for its flying buttresses and great rose windows?

Sport

1. In which sport is the Stanley Cup awarded?

2. Who was the first British football player to be knighted?

3. Which baseball ace held a record career total of 2,245 runs from retirement in 1928 until this record was surpassed in 2001?

4. What was the nickname of boxer, Joe Louis?

5. Which golfer carries the nickname 'The Great White Shark'?

6. Fatima Whitbread was the UK's first woman to achieve a world record in which athletics event?

7. Which female tennis player competed with Bobby Riggs in the game officially named 'Battle of the Sexes', in September 1973?

8. In which sport was Hashim Khan a several-times champion during the 1950s?

9. At which English football ground was there a disastrous fire in May 1985?

10. Finn, Lasse Virén, won four Olympic gold medals in what sport?

General Knowledge

1. Built in the 1880s, the Home Insurance building is acknowledged as the world's first skyscraper. In which American city was it built?

2. What type of creature is a drill?

3. Which German physician was the founder of homeopathy?

4. The archer is the symbol of which sign of the zodiac?

5. Name the American playwright who wrote 'Barefoot In The Park' and 'The Odd Couple'.

6. Which sign of the zodiac is represented by a lion?

7. By what acronym is radio detecting and ranging more commonly known?

8. An osier is what species of tree?

9. What kind of plant is a saguaro?

10. To depilate, means to remove what?

The Animal Kingdom

1   What breed of dog, a member of the greyhound family, is also known as Arabian hound, or gazelle hound?

_____

2   To which continent is the guanaco native?

_____

3   A mandrill is what type of creature?

_____

4   Porcine is the adjective for which animal?

_____

5   Which animals are called 'ships of the desert'?

_____

6   Through what on their body do fish breathe?

_____

7   Which American tree-dwelling marsupial reputedly deters predators by pretending to be dead?

_____

8   Which member of the cat family found on the American continent is otherwise known as puma, mountain lion, catamount and panther?

_____

9   What is the name of the hard resin, used in varnishing, which is produced on the bark of trees by insects?

_____

10 On which part of the body do grasshoppers have their ears?

Crime

1. By what nickname was mass-murderer David Berkowitz known?

2. What is the literal meaning of the word 'mafia'?

3. Which gangster gave his profession as 'Second hand furniture dealer' on his business cards?

4. Sing Sing prison is in which U.S. city?

5. What is the nickname of American bank robber Charles Floyd?

6. Who was President Nixon's Attorney General who was sent to prison as a result of the Watergate scandal?

7. In which Italian city was the 'Mona Lisa' recovered two years after it had been stolen from the Louvre in Paris?

8. What are double loops, radial loops, arches, whorls and ulna loops?

9. Which American anti-slave campaigner was hanged in 1869 after an abortive raid on the federal arsenal in Virginia?

10. Which country had a police force called the Tonton Macoutes?

Food and Drink

1. With regard to Mexican food, what name is given to a kind of thin pancake made from corn meal which takes its name from the Spanish for 'little round cake'?

2. In terms of modern science, particularly with regard to food products, what do the initials GM stand for?

3. What type of lettuce is named after the Greek island from which it originates?

4. What name is given to the many-seeded fruit of the tree Punica granatum?

5. By what name are the edible tubers of the plant Solanum tuberosum better known?

6. From which country do the drinks ouzo and retsina originate?

7. What name is given to the cocktail made up of gin, cointreau and lemon juice that first made its mark in London in 1919 but was perfected by Harry's Bar in Paris?

8. Having a high gluten content, which variety of wheat is the most commonly used in making pasta?

9. What type of citrus fruit is a shamouti?

10. What form of eating is John Montagu, an 18th century compulsive gambler, said to have invented because he refused to leave his gaming table for lunch?

Movie Music

1. Who composed the scores for 'The Planet of the Apes', 'Alien' and several 'Star Trek' movies?

2. Which French-born composer received awards for 'Lawrence of Arabia', 'Doctor Zhivago', 'A Passage to India' and 'Ghost'?

3. 'The Pink Panther' theme is possibly the best-remembered composition of which movie-music composer?

4. Who wrote scores for 'Midnight Cowboy', 'Dances with Wolves' and for several 'James Bond' movies?

5. Which German-born composer wrote scores for 'The Lion King', 'Gladiator', 'Pirates of the Caribbean' and 'The Simpsons Movie'?

6. Whose second piano concerto rose to fame in the wider world when it was used in the movie 'Brief Encounter'?

7. It's three rising notes on a solo trumpet is the instantly-recognised opening to Richard Strauss's 'Also Sprach Zarathustra'. To which 1968 movie was it the title theme?

8. Stephen Sondheim wrote the words, and Leonard Bernstein the music, for which 1961 movie?

9. The music of which Austrian composer appeared in the 1971 movie 'Death in Venice'?

10. Ennio Morricone composed the famous title theme to which trio of movies starring Clint Eastwood?

General Knowledge

1   The South American country of Venezuela gets its name from that of which city?

2   King Wenceslas, of Christmas carol fame, was a 10th century monarch of which historical country?

3   Which star is the brightest of any seen from Earth?

4   Which star is the brightest in the northern celestial hemisphere?

5   The Sami people are indigenous to the northern areas of which European region?

6   Dalmatian dogs have a tendency to suffer from defects in which sense organ?

7   What is the common name of the medical condition, hemicrania?

8   Which fictional monk/detective was created by the novelist Ellis Peters?

9   Of which famous work by Tchaikovsky did the composer say that it had "no artistic merit whatsoever"?

10 Robert O'Hara Burke extensively explored which country during the mid-nineteenth century?

Geography

1. Which island in the Tyrrhenian Sea is famous for its active volcano?

2. Which strait between the Aegean Sea and the Sea of Marmara was known in ancient times as the Hellespont?

3. Which town in southwest England, site of an annual rock music festival, is said to have connections with King Arthur and Joseph of Arimathea?

4. To which Italian city does the adjective Neapolitan relate?

5. What is the capital of the Czech Republic?

6. In which European country are the cities of Granada and Toledo?

7. Of which country is Yangtze Kiang or Chang Jiang the longest river?

8. The confluence of the White Nile and Blue Nile occurs at which African city?

9. In which city is the only royal palace in the United States?

10. The ancient city of Carthage is now in which country?

History

1. What was the name of the Allied offensive in the 1991 Gulf War?

2. Which city was the first capital of the Kingdom of Italy until 1865?

3. Felicitas Julia is the ancient name for which European capital city?

4. Which crop was affected by blight in 1846, leading to the Irish famine?

5. What, in the 16th and 17th centuries, was a 'pavane'?

6. In which country in 2000 did the Mayon volcano erupt?

7. What type of clock was invented by Levi Hutchins in 1787?

8. First sold in 1878, what became the registered trademark for petroleum jelly?

9. What, in 17th-century India, did the Emperor Shah Jahan build for his wife Mumtaz?

10. What was discovered by aviator James Angel while he was flying over Venezuela in 1935?

Literature

1 Which Shakespeare tragedy is subtitled 'The Prince of Denmark'?

_____

2 Who wrote the famous trilogy 'The Lord of the Rings'?

_____

3 Who is the Czechoslovakian-born British writer of the play 'The Real Thing'?

_____

4 Which Canadian province was colonized by Scottish poet Sir William Alexander?

_____

5 Which U.S. novelist wrote 'Something Happened'?

_____

6 Which Nobel prize-winning novelist wrote 'Humboldt's Gift' and 'The Dean's December'?

_____

7 Which German sociologist wrote 'The Protestant Ethic and the Spirit of Capitalism'?

_____

8 Which Nobel prize-winning Mexican poet died in 1998 at the age of 84?

_____

9 In the Hans Christian Andersen fairy story, what does the Ugly Duckling turn into?

_____

10 What was the name of the son of the novelist A.A. Milne who was the inspiration for his books?

General Knowledge

1   The songs 'Somewhere' and 'America' come from which 1957 musical play?

_____

2   La Palma and Gomera belong to which group of Atlantic islands?

_____

3   In which country are the Clearwater Lakes, created nearly 300 million years ago by two meteorite impacts?

_____

4   The 'Althing' is the name of the parliament of which country?

_____

5   The term 'Big Bang' was coined by which astronomer?

_____

6   Tiny Tim and Bob Cratchit are characters in which novel by Charles Dickens?

_____

7   On which part of the body would a surgeon perform a tracheotomy?

_____

8   The Cape Verde Islands lie off the westernmost point of which continent?

_____

9   Who created the 'Star Trek' TV series?

_____

10   'It was a bright cold day in April and the clocks were striking thirteen' is the opening line of which dystopian novel of 1949?

Art

1 In which U.S. city is the Guggenheim Museum?

2 Which Spanish artist painted 'Las Meninas'?

3 Which Spanish cubist artist was born José Victoriano Gonzalez?

4 Which member of Whistler's family features in his most famous painting?

5 Which controversial British artist is best known for works such as 'Mother and Child, Divided'?

6 To which English king did Hans Holbein the Younger become court painter?

7 What relation is painter Lucian Freud to psychoanalysis pioneer Sigmund Freud?

8 In which country was the painter Marc Chagall born?

9 Which artist, in his lifetime, sold only one of his own paintings, 'The Red Vineyard'?

10 What nationality was the painter Akseli Gallen-Kallela (1865-1931)?

Tunnels and Bridges

1 The Ponte Vecchio spans the Arno river in which Italian city?

_____

2 In which European country is the Gran Sasso road tunnel?

_____

3 The Verrazano Narrows Bridge is in which U.S. city?

_____

4 The Simplon rail tunnel runs under which mountain range?

_____

5 Due to its distinctive shape, which famous bridge is known locally as the 'coat-hanger'?

_____

6 The Charles Bridge crosses the Vltava river in which European capital?

_____

7 The Great Belt Bridge connects the islands of Funen and Zealand; in which country?

_____

8 In which Italian city is the famous Bridge of Sighs?

_____

9 The Eisenhower Memorial Tunnel in the U.S. state of Colorado, runs under which mountain range?

_____

10 The Lake Pontchartrain Causeway has a claim to being the world's longest bridge. In which U.S. state is it?

Sport and Games

1 What is the name of a stadium in which cycle races take place?

2 In a game of chess, which is the only piece that cannot move backwards?

3 Bing Crosby died in 1977 whilst playing golf in which country?

4 Who was Muhammad Ali's opponent in the fight known as the 'Thrilla In Manila'?

5 Which U.S. industrialist developed the current scoring system for contract bridge?

6 What does the O and J stand for in O. J. Simpson?

7 In tennis, what score comes after deuce?

8 Three American tennis stars lost to Björn Borg in Wimbledon men's singles finals. They were John McEnroe, Jimmy Connors and which other?

9 Which American rider won the 500cc world motor cycling championship in 1984, 1986, 1988 and 1989?

10 What is the name of the hourglass-shaped toy that is thrown and caught on a cord between the hands?

The Human Body

1 In which part of the body are the olfactory glands?

_____

2 What is the name of the muscular tissue in the eye that surrounds the pupil and is situated immediately in front of the lens?

_____

3 Which reading disability is popularly known as word blindness?

_____

4 What name is given to the state of being insensitive to pain, as induced artificially before operations?

_____

5 What is controlled by the lumbrical muscles?

_____

6 What name is given to the removal for examination of fluid surrounding an unborn baby in the mother's womb?

_____

7 What name is given to the threadlike structures in the nuclei of cells that carry genetic information?

_____

8 In which part of the body is the cochlea?

_____

9 What name is given to tissue damage caused by exposure to extreme cold?

_____

10 Which artery carries blood from the right ventricle to the lungs?

General Knowledge

1 Which instrument indicates the time by the direction or length of the shadow cast by an indicator mounted on a calibrated scale?

2 In which country is the North Magnetic Pole?

3 What do the initials P. G. stand for in the name of author P. G. Wodehouse?

4 From the Bible, what does the word 'Sabaoth' mean?

5 How do Deimos and Phobos, the two natural satellites of Mars, translate into English?

6 What is the more usual title of the Christmas carol 'Adeste Fideles'?

7 What kind of creature is a 'pipistrelle'?

8 Who did Colonel Claus von Stauffenberg attempt to assassinate in July 1944?

9 In which New York City district is Central Park?

10 In which European capital city are the Tivoli Gardens?

Entertainment

1 Usually, how many movements are there in a symphony?

2 Who, in a book by Anton Chekhov, are Olga, Masha and Irina?

3 Which World War I U.S. military hero, originally a conscientious objector, was played on-screen by Gary Cooper?

4 Who became Annie's guardian in the story of 'Little Orphan Annie'?

5 In the poem by Edward Lear, for how long did the owl and the pussycat sail before reaching land?

6 Which character was played by Ted Danson in 'Cheers'?

7 Which Shakespeare character's last words are: "The rest is silence."?

8 Who played Jason Colby in 'The Colbys'?

9 What flower did singer Billie Holiday always wear in the right side of her hair?

10 What is the name of Mr Spock's home planet in 'Star Trek'?

Pop Music

1 The album 'Let's Dance' was a hit for ___?

2 Which group released the albums 'Dirty Deeds Done Dirt Cheap' and 'For Those About To Rock' in 1981?

3 In 1984 which group released the album 'Parade'?

4 Who had a hit album called 'She Works Hard For The Money' in 1983?

5 Who were 'So Excited!' in 1982?

6 Who came on a 'Ship Arriving Too Late To Save A Drowning Witch' in 1982?

7 Which group asked 'Who's Better, Who's Best' in 1988?

8 Whose 1980 album was entitled 'Women and Children First'?

9 Who made 'False Accusations' in 1985?

10 Which American group had a hit in 1983 with 'Allies'?

Movies

1 Which 1995 movie starred Tim Daly as a perfume developer and Sean Young as his female alter-ego?

2 Which ripping 1966 Alfred Hitchcock movie starred Paul Newman and Julie Andrews?

3 Who starred as Lawrence of Arabia in David Lean's 1962 movie of that name?

4 Which 1995 movie starred Keith Carradine and Daryl Hannah as psychotic parents?

5 Who played the title role in the movie 'Johnny Mnemonic'?

6 Who played Aunty, mistress of Bartertown, in 'Mad Max Beyond Thunderdome'?

7 Which 1996 movie starred Robin Williams and a host of jungle creatures?

8 Who starred as Fast Eddie Felson in the movie 'The Hustler'?

9 Which horror actor's performances included the Monster in 1935's 'Bride of Frankenstein' and 1939's 'Son of Frankenstein'?

10 Which 'Top Gun' star played a political activist in the 1988 movie 'The House on Carroll Street'?

General Knowledge

1 Which acid gives lemons and limes their sharp taste?

2 Which Roman emperor had both his wife and his mother executed?

3 Known as Helsingfors during the time of Swedish rule, what is the present-day name of this capital city?

4 By population, which is the largest city of the U.S.A.?

5 What term is used for a timber, steel or stone supporting beam over a door or window opening?

6 Who was head of the Federal Bureau of Investigation (FBI) from 1935 until his death in 1972?

7 Of the four 'Blackadder' TV series, which was set during the time of World War I?

8 Actor, Nicolas Cage is a nephew of which film director?

9 Pretoria is the administrative capital of which country?

10 According to the saying, to which capital city do 'all roads lead'?

History

1 Diana, Princess of Wales died in which month of 1997?

2 Which Albanian-born humanitarian and Nobel Peace Prize winner died on the 5th September 1997?

3 What German phrase was displayed at the entrance to concentration camps during the 1930s-40s?

4 Which Canadian city was founded by Champlain in 1608?

5 Religious leader Brigham Young founded which U.S. city in the 1840s?

6 Which great Zulu chieftain and conqueror died in 1828?

7 In July 1988 the American cruiser 'U.S.S. Vincennes' accidentally shot down a civilian airliner belonging to which country?

8 Which dictator and his wife were executed on Christmas Day 1989?

9 What name is given to Monday 1st October 1987 when stock markets around the world crashed?

10 Which patriot of the American Revolution was the subject of an 1860 poem by Longfellow?

U.S. TV Comedy

1   Who was the talking horse of the 1960s eponymously-titled TV series?

2   In which 1980s series did Robert Guillaume play the part of a butler 'with attitude'?

3   Ted Danson played barman, Sam Malone, in which series?

4   Who played the part of Phoebe Buffay in 'Friends'?

5   What was the name of the taxi company in the 1980s hit series, 'Taxi'?

6   Which odd family, comprising Herman, Lily, Grandpa, Marilyn and Eddie, lived at 1313 Mockingbird Lane?

7   In the hit series 'The Simpsons' what is the first name of Mr Burns' personal assistant, Smithers?

8   Which 1960s series, starring Elizabeth Montgomery as Samantha Stephens, was reworked into a 2005 film with Nicole Kidman in the same role?

9   The Huxtable family featured in which long-running series?

10   In which 2003 series does Michael, who seems to be the only sane person in the Bluth family, constantly strive to save other family-members from themselves?

Mythology

1 In Arthurian legend, which knight of the Round Table was the son of King Lot?

2 Who was the god of war in Greek mythology?

3 In Greek mythology, who was the leader of the Argonauts?

4 Which winged horse in Greek mythology sprang from the blood of Medusa?

5 What was the name of King Arthur's sword?

6 Who was the Greek god of sleep, called Somnus by the Romans?

7 Which planet is named after the Roman god of the sea?

8 In Greek mythology, who was Hector's wife who was taken as a concubine by Achilles's son?

9 What did the Romans call the Greek goddess, Aphrodite?

10 Which day of the week was named after the mythological son of Woden?

Famous Buildings

1   Which great mosque in Istanbul was built by Sultan Ahmed the First in the early seventeenth century?

_____

2   The Paris landmark that houses the main library and museum of modern art is named after which former French president?

_____

3   The Petronas Towers are in which Asian capital city?

_____

4   The Hermitage Museum is in which Russian city?

_____

5   In which U.S. city is the 1,450 feet high Wills Tower (formerly called the Sears Tower)?

_____

6   Which Toronto landmark was, at the time of its completion in 1976, the world's tallest tower?

_____

7   Substantially damaged in 1945 but subsequently restored, in which European city is St Stephen's Cathedral?

_____

8   The Burj Khalifa is the world's tallest building. In which city is it sited?

_____

9   The Taj Mahal stands in which Indian city?

_____

10 Which triangular-plan New York building, sited at the intersection of three main streets, was one of the city's first skyscrapers?

General Knowledge

1 Which type of Chinese food translates as 'bits and pieces'?

_____

2 Heinrich Himmler was the leader of which German Nazi organization?

_____

3 Who is the ferryman of Greek mythology who carries the souls of the dead across the River Styx?

_____

4 What is the vegetable ingredient in the dish, eggs florentine?

_____

5 Which sailor-hero of Middle Eastern fiction is carried off by a gigantic bird, the Roc?

_____

6 In Greek mythology, who were the giant offspring of Gaius and Uranus that ruled the Earth?

_____

7 In which African country is the port of Tobruk?

_____

8 Killed by Achilles in the Trojan War, who was the eldest son of King Priam?

_____

9 In the poem by Robert Burns, who is chased by witches as he rides home on a stormy night?

_____

10 What is the English name for the 'Ponti di Sospiri', the noted bridge in Venice?

Music of the 70s

1 In 1976 'Songs in the Key of Life' was whose album?

_____

2 Which group released the album 'Toys in the Attic' in 1975?

_____

3 Which group released, in 1975, the album 'That's The Way Of The World'?

_____

4 Whose was the album 'The Stranger' released in 1977?

_____

5 1974 heard an album 'Tubular Bells' being played everywhere. By whom was it released?

_____

6 Who was responsible for the 1979 album 'The Wall'?

_____

7 Whose was the 1973 album 'Goats Head Soup'?

_____

8 Which group produced the 1971 album 'Coal Miner's Daughter'?

_____

9 In 1972 David Bowie issued an album which caught the imagination of a generation. What was it called?

_____

10 Who had an absolutely massive hit in 1970 with 'Close To You'?

Science

1 In geometry, what name is given to a quarter of the circumference of a circle?

2 What name is given to an instrument used for measuring the relative density of a liquid?

3 Which narcotic drug is obtained from opium and used in medicine for the relief of severe pain?

4 What are the three main categories into which rocks are divided?

5 Name the place in northern Italy where in 1976 a leak from the chemical works contaminated the surrounding area, killing animals and causing people to suffer from skin disorders and other ailments.

6 Which SI unit of electric charge is represented by the symbol C?

7 Which type of weapon is represented by the abbreviation ICBM?

8 Which scientific term describes the bending of a beam of light as it passes from one medium to another?

9 In medicine, aetiology or etiology is the study of what?

10 What name is given to the diode valve which is the source of microwaves in a microwave oven?

ANSWERS

Round 1   1 The foot, 2 The Atlantic, 3 Death of the firstborn, 4 Amman (capital of Jordan), 5 225, 6 Pisces, Cancer and Scorpio, 7 A (black) star, 8 Trees, 9 India and Burma (Myanmar), 10 Janus.

Round 2   1 Melon, 2 Iceland, 3 Peanut, 4 Mandarin orange and sweet orange, 5 Peach, 6 Bolivia, 7 Pomelo, 8 Tomato, 9 Apple, 10 Any fruit with a fleshy exterior and a single stone or kernel inside.

Round 3   1 Jim Clark, 2 Rod Laver, 3 Kristin Otto, 4 Joe DiMaggio, 5 Captain Matthew Webb, 6 Colombian, 7 Lou Gehrig, 8 New York, 9 Flic-flac, 10 Rocky Marciano.

Round 4   1 A sail, 2 Rudolf Diesel, 3 Aeroflot, 4 The 'Hindenburg', 5 Flying Fortress, 6 Atlantic, 7 Venice, 8 Gottlieb Daimler, 9 Thomas Cook, 10 'Titanic'.

Round 5   1 Epiphany, 2 John Nelson Darby, 3 Limbo, 4 Ganges, 5 William Penn, 6 Martin Luther King Jr., 7 Loreto, 8 The Salvation Army, 9 Druidism, 10 Mecca.

Round 6   1 February, 2 Ufology, 3 Mice, 4 Heights, 5 Cape Town, 6 Ayers Rock, 7 Pants (trousers) or jeans, 8 Goat, 9 Modem, 10 Culottes.

Round 7   1 Sierra Nevada, 2 Missouri, 3 Mexico, 4 On the Statue of Liberty, 5 Burundi, 6 Nebraska, 7 Michigan, 8 Pacific Ocean, 9 Rhode Island, 10 Gibraltar.

Round 8   1 Beethoven, 2 Choral singer, member of choir, 3 'Air on the G String', 4 Amati, 5 'El Amor Brujo' ('Love the Magician'), 6 The 'Andante Cantabile', 7 'Peer Gynt', 8 In the modern style, 9 'The William Tell Overture', 10 Wagner.

Round 9   1 Pepsi Cola, 2 Retsina, 3 Cuba, 4 Horse, 5 Double basses, 6 1789, 7 The can-opener was invented around 1855, 8 Potassium, 9 U.S.A, 10 France.

Round 10 1 Helena Bonham Carter, 2 Warren Beatty, 3 'Hanging Up', 4 Christopher Walken, 5 Jack Nicholson, 6 Charles Bronson, 7 Washington Irving, 8 'Play Misty for Me', 9 An octopus, 10 Darth Vader.

Round 11 1 Coyote, 2 Bullfrog, 3 Pelican, 4 Seal, 5 Falcon, 6 Duck, 7 Parr, 8 Gills, 9 Jellyfish, 10 Firefly.

Round 12 1 1962, 2 Crimean War, 3 Coventry, 4 Germany and Holland, 5 Henry VIII, 6 Martin Luther King , 7 Human stupidity, 8 It's the only one left, 9 Italy, 10 Crete.

Round 13 1 Nimbus, 2 Yale, 3 Vernal, 4 Gothenburg, 5 Typhoons, 6 Trigonometry, 7 Saluki, 8 Sirocco, 9 The wolf, 10 A pipe of peace.

Round 14 1 Claude Monet, 2 L.S. Lowry, 3 Edouard Manet, 4 Photography, 5 Vincent van Gogh, 6 Ecce Homo, 7 Claude Monet, 8 Grinling Gibbons, 9 Campbell's, 10 Raphael.

Round 15 1 Aesop, 2 Jacob and Wilhelm, 3 Sancho Panza, 4 Jane, 5 Thomas Mann, 6 Bram Stoker, 7 Jack Kerouac, 8 Jean Cocteau, 9 John, 10 Graham Greene.

Round 16 1 Juan Carlos I of Spain, 2 Walker, 3 Spain, 4 General Augusto Pinochet, 5 Pakistan, 6 Chaim Weizmann, 7 Spain, 8 Seattle, 9 The Philippines, 10 A lion.

Round 17 1 Brazil, 2 Romania, 3 Japan, 4 Peru, 5 Kaiser, 6 Free French, 6 Pompey the Great, 8 Pol Pot, 9 Austria, 10 7th.

Round 18 1 Guilder, 2 Dahlia, 3 Egypt, 4 1976, 5 Casablanca, 6 Abraham Lincoln, 7 Donna Karan New York, 8 Lisa Marie, 9 Internet Service Provider, 10 Blue.

ANSWERS

Round 19   1 Los Angeles, 2 John Lennon, 3 Stockholm, 4 Idlewild, 5 Jan Smuts, 6 Iceland, 7 Milan, 8 Houston, 9 Canada, 10 London Heathrow.

Round 20   1 Dionysus, 2 Orpheus, 3 Osiris, 4 Snakes, 5 Vesta, 6 Nike, 7 Apples, 8 Apollo, 9 Daphne, 10 Sirens.

Round 21   1 W.C. Handy, 2 A Spanish dance in 3/4 time, usually slow and in a minor key, 3 Larry Adler, 4 Richard Addinsell, 5 Bayreuth, 6 'My Country 'tis of Thee', 7 Graceful, 8 Offenbach, 9 Softly, 10 Earl 'Fatha' Hines.

Round 22   1 The Holy Grail, 2 Braemar, 3 Canterbury, 4 Steel, 5 Nevada, 6 Ireland, 7 Prosthetics, 8 Red and violet, 9 Dutch, 10 Zinc.

Round 23   1 Salt, 2 Pewter, 3 Metal fatigue, 4 Velocity, 5 Möbius strip, 6 Latex, 7 Water, 8 Haematite, 9 California, 10 Verdigris.

Round 24   1 Holiday Inn, 2 La Guardia, 3 Entebbe, 4 Marco Polo, 5 Lady Godiva, 6 Amphitheatre, 7 Ferdinand V and Isabella I, 8 Saint Bartholomew, 9 Hannibal, 10 Ides.

Round 25   1 The Olympics, 2 Patty Berg, 3 They were all female, 4 Denver, 5 Albatross, 6 Meadowlark, 7 Skiing, 8 Pistol shooting, 9 Fencing, 10 The Yankee Stadium.

Round 26   1 Damsel fly, 2 Tsetse fly, 3 Termite, 4 Beetles, 5 Cicadas, 6 Human flea, 7 The locust, 8 Horse fly, 9 Beetle, 10 A butterfly.

Round 27   1 Taj Mahal, 2 Athens, 3 Constantine, 4 Paper, 5 Chinese, 6 Dog, 7 Nine, 8 Absent without leave, 9 Italy, 10 London Bridge.

Round 28   1 Iran and Iraq, 2 Saskatchewan, 3 Victoria, 4 Rotterdam, 5 Colon, 6 A glacier, 7 Adige, 8 Messina, 9 Kansas, 10 Utah.

ANSWERS

Round 29   1 Coney, 2 Greece, 3 Puerto Rico, 4 Canary Islands, 5 Cook Strait, 6 Cephalonia, 7 Galapagos, 8 Ellis Island, 9 Seychelles, 10 Utopia.

Round 30   1 'Silk Stockings', 2 '8MM', 3 'Besieged', 4 Plunkett and Macleane, 5 John Travolta, 6 Lt. Frank Drebin, 7 'Pleasantville', 8 Mel Gibson, 9 'Ishtar', 10 'The Last Detail'.

Round 31   1 Washington DC, 2 Equivalent to one million tons of TNT, 3 Anemone, 4 Venice, 5 Doris Day, 6 Solidarity, 7 Italy, 8 Batman and Robin, 9 M.C. Escher, 10 St Paul.

Round 32   1 Sodom and Gomorrah, 2 Adam, 3 Raven, 4 Genesis, 5 Aaron, 6 Jonathan, 7 Rachel, 8 'The Vulgate', 9 Obadiah, 10 Barabbas.

Round 33   1 The Temptations, 2 Thin Lizzy, 3 Yes, 4 Marc Bolan and T. Rex, 5 'Let It Be', 6 Blondie, 7 The Sex Pistols, 8 Carlos Santana, 9 Queen, 10 Iggy Pop.

Round 34   1 Tetanus, 2 Retina, 3 Pelvis, 4 Chickenpox, 5 White blood cells, 6 Goitre, 7 Nerves, 8 Tears, 9 The brain, 10 Insulin.

Round 35   1 Lana Turner, 2 William Hurt, 3 Savinien, 4 Richard Brinsley Sheridan, 5 Hamelin, 6 Falsetto, 7 The Andrews Sisters, 8 Kathy Bates, 9 Charlie Rich, 10 Mark Twain.

Round 36   1 Denmark, 2 Portuguese, 3 Martin Luther King, 4 Lapland, 5 Hornet, 6 France, 7 Nucleus, 8 Green, 9 'The Flying Dutchman', 10 Italy.

Round 37   1 Heloise, 2 Boutros Boutros-Ghali, 3 Charles Martel, 4 Guillotine, 5 Dallas, 6 Belgium, 7 Charlotte Corday, 8 Aberfan, 9 Istanbul, 10 Abacus.

Round 38   1 Sideshow Bob, 2 The Leftorium, 3 Monorail, 4 Maude, 5 Patty and Selma, 6 The Android's Dungeon, 7 Waylon Smithers, 8 Ralph, 9 Kent Brockman, 10 Does whatever a spider-pig does.

Round 39   1 Edward Gibbon, 2 E.B. White, 3 Rebecca West, 4 Casanova, 5 S.J. Perelman, 6 Mary Ann Evans, 7 J.M. Synge, 8 Ludwig Wittgenstein, 9 Alexandre Dumas, 10 O. Henry.

Round 40   1 Mulberry, 2 Buster Keaton, 3 Orville and Wilbur, 4 120, 5 Minnehaha, 6 'West Side Story', 7 Albania, 8 Florence, 9 Hans Holbein the Younger, 10 Heraklion.

Round 41   1 Twelve, 2 Five, 3 Nine, 4 41, 5 2,3,5,7, 6 Eleven, 7 The Three Graces, 8 Charity, 9 Temperaments, 10 Jewish.

Round 42   1 The Spanish Civil War, 2 The American Civil War, 3 Enigma, 4 Auschwitz, 5 Gran Chaco, 6 1898, 7 Joseph Goebbels, 8 Aircraft, 9 Agamemnon, 10 New Mexico.

Round 43   1 Laurel and Hardy, 2 Groucho, 3 Charlie Chaplin, 4 Billy Wilder, 5 George Burns, 6 Rich Hall, 7 Matt Groening, 8 Allan Sherman, 9 Mel Brooks, 10 Gene Wilder.

Round 44   1 The Inferno, 2 Niki Lauda, 3 Althea Gibson, 4 Three under, 5 Eddie the Eagle, 6 Berlin 1936, 7 Africa, 8 Basketball, 9 Uruguay, 10 Muhammad Ali.

Round 45   1 Ontario, 2 Kalashnikov, 3 Red and blue, 4 Thalidomide, 5 Tripoli, 6 Pamela Lyndon, 7 Six, 8 France, 9 50, 10 Sony.

Round 46   1 Play frankly, boldly, 2 Diminishing and slowing, 3 'Elijah', 4 A characteristic of a friend of the composer, 5 'Pictures at an Exhibition', 6 Emmanuel Chabriere, 7 George Frederick Handel, 8 'Roman Festivals', 9 Maurice Ravel, 10 Gian-Carlo Menotti.

ANSWERS

Round 47 1 Transistor, 2 Photographic film, 3 Ornithology, 4 Mycology, 5 Danish, 6 Chromium, 7 Phylum, 8 Photosynthesis, 9 Hydrogen, 10 Lead.

Round 48 1 France, Belgium and Luxembourg, 2 Paraguay, 3 Maine, 4 The Nile, 5 Prairie Provinces, 6 Canada, 7 Iran, 8 Switzerland, 9 Taiwan, 10 Atlantic Ocean.

Round 49 1 Glen Miller, 2 Russia, 3 Denmark, 4 Irving Berlin, 5 Boy Scouts, 6 Tierra del Fuego, 7 The Netherlands, 8 Goat, 9 737, 10 Macau.

Round 50 1 Microwave oven, 2 Luger, 3 Venice, 4 Stasi, 5 Central Park, 6 Diogenes, 7 Rosenberg, 8 Potlatch, 9 Davy Crockett, 10 Nostradamus.

Round 51 1 Billy Bob Thornton, 2 'She's All That', 3 'Petulia', 4 'The Family Man', 5 'Uptown Saturday Night', 6 'Unbreakable', 7 Rod Steiger, 8 'The Way We Were', 9 '84 Charing Cross Road', 10 'Meet the Applegates'.

Round 52 1 Ugli, 2 Ginger, 3 Onion, 4 Fenugreek, 5 Parsley, 6 Sugar, 7 Casein, 8 Potatoes, 9 Spaghetti, 10 Textured Vegetable Protein.

Round 53 1 'Pagliacci', 2 Morecambe and Wise, 3 Starsky and Hutch, 4 Danish, 5 The Righteous Brothers, 6 Romeo and Juliet, 7 Simon & Garfunkel, 8 Hansel and Gretel, 9 Wallace and Gromit, 10 Rosencrantz and Guildenstern.

Round 54 1 Chess, 2 Australia, 3 Hugh Hefner, 4 The peacemaker, 5 Sapphire, 6 Libra, 7 Covetousness, 8 Green, 9 El Dorado, 10 Italy.

Round 55 1 Palindrome, 2 Citadel, 3 Plumbing, 4 A diaper, 5 Keiron, 6 The English Channel, 7 Oxymoron, 8 French, 9 Mumbo Jumbo, 10 Femme Fatale.

Round 56   1 Seamus Heaney, 2 Hiawatha, 3 Robert Burns, 4 Ted Hughes, 5 Dylan Thomas, 6 John Milton, 7 Juvenal, 8 Edgar Allan Poe, 9 George Herbert, 10 Ezra Pound.

Round 57   1 Egypt, 2 Epiphany, 3 1st November, 4 St. Nicholas, 5 Constantine, 6 Sun Myung Moon, 7 South Korea, 8 Iran, 9 Adventists, 10 Louis IX.

Round 58   1 Israel, 2 Carbon monoxide, 3 Venezuela, 4 Fidel Castro, 5 Make or build a nest, 6 Albert Einstein, 7 Antelope, 8 Rockets, 9 Hemp, 10 Windows.

Round 59   1 Paul McCartney, 2 Terracotta, 3 Guitar, 4 Leadbelly, 5 'Nature Boy', 6 Neil Young, 7 'Size Isn't Everything', 8 Shirley Bassey, 9 Pink Floyd, 10 The Pogues.

Round 60   1 Meteors, 2 Caterpillar, 3 Nectar, 4 Marsupials, 5 Condor, 6 Tench, 7 Invertebrate, 8 Venom, 9 Its whiskers, 10 Puffin.

Round 61   1 Flora, 2 Parthenon, 3 Eros, 4 Hermes, 5 Three, 6 Nine, 7 Camelot, 8 Titans, 9 Leprechaun, 10 Morgan le Fay.

Round 62   1 Norway, 2 Crucifixion, 3 Samuel Pepys, 4 Gebhard von Blücher, 5 Ass's milk, 6 Tutankhamen, 7 Adolf Hitler, 8 He was a passenger on the 'Titanic', 9 Arc de Triomphe, 10 Mammoth.

Round 63   1 Louis XVI, 2 Caligula, 3 Shipping, 4 File Transfer Protocol, 5 Read Only Memory, 6 Mithraism, 7 Janet Reno, 8 Fay Wray, 9 Local Area Network, 10 The Mediterranean Sea.

Round 64   1 A goat carcass, 2 A 90 km cross-country ski-race, 3 Tennis, 4 Usain Bolt, 5 Finnish (born in Sweden), 6 1916, 1940, 1944, 7 Shergar, 8 Muhammad Ali and Joe Frazier, 9 Portugal, 10 Manchester United.

Round 65   1 'Oliver Twist', 2 Truman Capote, 3 Thomas Carlyle, 4 Katherine Mansfield, 5 Sturm und Drang, 6 Stephen Crane, 7 Alberto Moravia, 8 John le Carré, 9 Philip Roth, 10 James Baldwin.

Round 66   1 Spica, 2 1980s, 3 Aquarius, 4 Taurus, 5 Space Transportation System, 6 Mars, 7 100%, 8 Crux, 9 John Glenn, 10 Laika.

Round 67   1 Suzi Quatro, 2 South America, 3 Hedgehog, 4 Greta Garbo, 5 Jerusalem, 6 Hyde Park, 7 Diamond, 8 The Pacific, 9 Pakistan, 10 Austria and Italy.

Round 68   1 The Rockies, 2 Switzerland, 3 Canada, 4 Mount Parnassus, 5 Lille, 6 Himalayas, 7 River Tagus, 8 Canada and U.S.A., 9 The Arno, 10 Rio Grande.

Round 69   1 Ehud Barak, 2 Kenya, 3 Michael Dukakis, 4 Jefferson Davis, 5 Corazon Aquino, 6 Andrew Volstead, 7 Dwight D. Eisenhower, 8 Niccolo Machiavelli, 9 New York, 10 Million Man March.

Round 70   1 Arizona, 2 Cork, 3 Shanghai, 4 Burma, 5 Strait of Messina, 6 Poland, 7 Wisconsin, 8 Bay of Biscay, 9 Kyoto, 10 Tierra del Fuego.

Round 71   1 'Your Friends and Neighbors', 2 'Macao', 3 'Eyes of Laura Mars', 4 'The Object of Beauty', 5 Gregory Peck, 6 'Perfect', 7 Brad Pitt, 8 Kathy Bates, 9 Whoopi Goldberg, 10 'Colors'.

Round 72   1 Nirvana, 2 The Black Sea, 3 Piccolo, 4 Bassoon, 5 Hungary, 6 Hindu, 7 South Carolina, 8 Mickey Mouse, 9 Mascagni, 10 Tree.

Round 73   1 The Cars, 2 Kiss, 3 The Beatles, 4 Booker T. and the MGs, 5 'Fifth Dimension', 6 Donovan, 7 'Strange Days', 8 Bob Dylan, 9 Barry White, 10 Talking Heads.

Round 74 1 Portuguese, 2 Julius and Ethel Rosenberg, 3 Pierre de Fermat, 4 Rudolph Valentino, 5 Spandau, 6 Aristotle Onassis, 7 Jakarta, 8 Nero, 9 French Revolution, 10 Annie Oakley.

Round 75 1 Turtle, 2 Wasps, 3 Osprey, 4 Lovebirds, 5 Cobra, 6 Okapi, 7 Crocodile, 8 Swan, 9 Fumigation, 10 Catfish.

Round 76 1 180, 2 London School of Economics, 3 Mexico, 4 Russia, 5 Boreas, 6 'She Loves You', 7 Copenhagen, 8 Degrees Celsius to Fahrenheit, 9 First ever drive-in cinema, 10 Model T Ford.

Round 77 1 Flash Gordon, 2 Little Richard, 3 Athens, 4 'Sleeper', 5 Perry Como, 6 Canada, 7 "Elvis has left the building", 8 Munich, 9 'When You Wish Upon a Star', 10 Kathy Kane.

Round 78 1 Chopin, 2 Copland, 3 'El Amor Brujo', 4 'The Nutcracker', 5 'The Rite of Spring', 6 'Coppelia', 7 Khachaturian, 8 Stravinsky, 9 Argentinian, 10 'Romeo and Juliet'.

Round 79 1 Computer-Aided Design, 2 IBM, 3 Hewlett-Packard, 4 Pixels or megapixels, 5 ENIAC, 6 Intel, 7 'Toy Story', 8 Random-Access Memory, 9 A motherboard, 10 1985.

Round 80 1 Vladivostok, 2 Atlanta, 3 St. Christopher, 4 The Spitfire, 5 H.M.S. 'Beagle', 6 Turkey, 7 Igor Sikorsky, 8 U.S.S. 'Nautilus', 9 Model A, 10 An all-metal airplane.

Round 81 1 Gianni Versace, 2 Gregorian calendar, 3 Nitrogen, 4 Ireland, 5 Interpol, 6 'Romeo and Juliet', 7 Dopey, 8 David Ben-Gurion, 9 Jupiter, 10 Agrippina.

Round 82 1 A puck, 2 Bishop, 3 John McEnroe, 4 The game of baseball, 5 Italy, 6 Six, 7 Canada, 8 Vitas Gerulaitis, 9 Siena, 10 Gary Kasparov.

Round 83 1 Gabriel and Michael, 2 Armageddon, 3 The Ten Commandments, 4 Genesis, 5 Belshazzar, 6 969, 7 Gopher wood, 8 Shadrach, Meshach and Abednego, 9 He turned water into wine, 10 The Pentateuch.

Round 84 1 Physics, 2 Impedance, 3 Meteor showers, 4 Acid rain, 5 Steel, 6 Geometry, 7 Megaton, 8 Molecule, 9 Chloroform, 10 1920s.

Round 85 1 E Pluribus Unum, 2 The skull, 3 If Allah wills it, 4 Marlon Brando, 5 River Plate, 6 American, 7 Atlantic, 8 The Appian Way, 9 Acupuncture, 10 Philosopher's stone.

Round 86 1 14th, 2 Livia Drusilla, 3 Cynics, 4 Plato, 5 Italy, 6 Siamese twins, 7 Weimar Republic, 8 Ulrike Meinhof, 9 The Red Army Faction, 10 Sir John Barbirolli.

Round 87 1 Roy Eldridge, 2 Art Tatum, 3 Dave Brubeck, 4 Kai Winding, 5 Django Rheinhardt, 6 Gato Barbieri, 7 Sandy Brown, 8 Thelonius Monk, 9 James P. Johnson, 10 Jan Garbarek.

Round 88 1 Laszlo Biro, 2 Triode, 3 German, 4 Telephone, 5 Moog, 6 Sextant, 7 Celluloid, 8 Hiram S. Maxim, 9 Eli Whitney, 10 Jacques Cousteau.

Round 89 1 'Magnificent Obsession', 2 Tommy Steele, 3 'Affliction', 4 'See No Evil, Hear No Evil', 5 Woody Allen, 6 'Narrow Margin', 7 Fred Astaire, 8 'Major League', 9 Julianne Moore, 10 Mimi Rogers.

Round 90 1 Nimitz, 2 ETA, 3 Yugoslavia, 4 Intifada, 5 Charlemagne, 6 Idi Amin, 7 Robert Redford, 8 Cleopatra, 9 Denmark, 10 The hardness of minerals.

Round 91 1 The Danube, 2 Alaska, 3 Linz, 4 Kyushu, 5 Borneo, 6 Aborigines, 7 Cajuns, 8 New Brunswick, 9 Amsterdam, 10 Venice.

ANSWERS

Round 92   1 H.G. Wells, 2 Cyrano de Bergerac, 3 'I'm Talking About Jerusalem', 4 'The Lost Generation', 5 Alexander Pope, 6 Ferenc Molnar, 7 Douglas Adams, 8 'The Forsyte Saga', 9 Richard Gordon, 10 Nigerian.

Round 93   1 The Netherlands, 2 Paul Gauguin, 3 A clock, 4 Goya, 5 Ottawa, 6 Pride, 7 Rodin, 8 Dutch, 9 Pablo, 10 Giotto.

Round 94   1 Organization of Petroleum Exporting Countries, 2 F. Scott Fitzgerald, 3 'The Comedy of Errors', 4 'The King and I', 5 Bill Haley and his Comets, 6 Christa McAuliffe, 7 Hollywood, 8 Luke Skywalker, 9 Violin, 10 Westerns.

Round 95   1 S.S. 'Athenia', 2 'Graf Spee', 3 The Maginot Line, 4 Finland, 5 Munich, 6 Neville Chamberlain, 7 Blitzkrieg (lightning war), 8 First Lord of the Admiralty, 9 Albania, 10 London.

Round 96   1 Tadpole, 2 Lizard, 3 Horse, 4 Walrus, 5 Sloth, 6 Horse, 7 Orangutan, 8 Kookaburra, 9 Firefly, 10 Woodlice.

Round 97   1 Green, 2 Cheese, 3 Cod, 4 Retsina, 5 Orange and tangerine, 6 Almonds, 7 Pesto, 8 Blackcurrants, 9 Italy, 10 Poland.

Round 98   1 Hiroshima (the Enola Gay was a plane, and the Little Boy was an atom bomb), 2 Russia, 3 Finland, 4 Sweden, 5 Iraq invaded Kuwait, 6 Spanish Flu, 7 1917, 8 Sputnik 1, 9 Winston Churchill, 10 George Washington.

Round 99   1 A sphere, flattened at the poles, 2 Alligator, 3 Cambodia, 4 Ethiopia, 5 Shin Bet, 6 The Appian Way, 7 Twelve, 8 Portugal, 9 Between 50 and 58, 10 Baader-Meinhof.

Round 100   1 'Also Sprach Zarathustra', 2 Michael Tippett, 3 Gyorgy Ligeti, 4 'Divertissement', 5 John Adams, 6 Carreras, 7 Sir Simon Rattle, 8 Henryk Gorecki, 9 Jascha Heifetz, 10 Right.

Round 101   1 Athens, 1896, 2 Four and a half miles, 3 Stan Smith, 4 Snowboarding, 5 Pele, 6 Shane Gould, 7 Henry Cooper, 8 Swimming, cycling and running, 9 Greyhound racing, 10 Hamburg.

Round 102   1 Malaysia, 2 Japan, 3 Switzerland, 4 Spain, 5 South Africa, 6 Latvia, 7 Liechtenstein, 8 Uganda, 9 Morocco, 10 Chile.

Round 103   1 Sturgeon, 2 Decibels, 3 Winds, 4 The Dow-Jones index, 5 Martin Freeman, 6 Medina, 7 King Arthur, 8 Stalingrad, 9 Anthracite, 10 Cobra.

Round 104   1 Andromeda, 2 Merlin, 3 Narcissus, 4 Mars, 5 Ariadne, 6 A Gorgon, 7 Penates, 8 Niobe, 9 Mount Parnassus, 10 Achilles.

Round 105   1 H.M.S. 'Victory', 2 'Santa Maria', 3 'General Belgrano', 4 'Mary Celeste', 5 'Exxon Valdez', 6 U.S.S. 'Enterprise', 7 U.S.S. 'Nautilus', 8 France, 9 'Wilhelm Gustloff', 10 Both were naval ships that sank, were later raised, and are now on public display.

Round 106   1 Sunlight, 2 Cairo, 3 Heliosphere, 4 Helios, 5 Heliogram, 6 Helium, 7 Heliotrope, 8 Helioscope, 9 Heliology, 10 Carl Nielsen.

Round 107   1 Egypt, 2 March, 3 Pyrenees, 4 St. Peter, 5 St. Francis Xavier, 6 The River Ganges, 7 'Edict of Nantes', 8 The Great Awakening, 9 Zoroastrianism, 10 Jainism.

Round 108   1 Let the buyer beware, 2 Elvis Presley, 3 South Fork, 4 A park, 5 Switzerland, 6 'Hamlet', 7 14, 8 Edison, 9 'Othello', 10 Liberace.

Round 109   1 Every 76 years, 2 Transformer, 3 Albert Einstein, 4 Ytterbium, 5 Hypothermia, 6 Plumbum, 7 Arcturus, 8 Kiloton, 9 Israel, 10 Modem.

ANSWERS

Round 110 1 Chicago, 2 'The Long March', 3 Muskets, 4 The Battle of Britain, 5 Air traffic controllers, 6 Scrofula, 7 Abbey Theatre, 8 Anne Frank, 9 Munich, 10 Halifax.

Round 111 1 'Tommy Boy', 2 Sean Connery, 3 Rex Harrison, 4 Denzel Washington, 5 Tina Turner, 6 'The Scarlet Letter', 7 'The Basketball Diaries', 8 Stanley Kubrick, 9 Liza Minnelli, 10 Spencer Tracy.

Round 112 1 Sicily, 2 Gresham's Law, 3 Lower, 4 Loire, 5 Tokyo, 6 Tom Thumb, 7 Belle, 8 Anastasia, 9 Alcock and Brown, 10 Philip of Macedonia.

Round 113 1 k.d. lang, 2 Led Zeppelin, 3 Lionel Richie, 4 The Rolling Stones, 5 Sade, 6 The Verve, 7 'Like A Virgin', 8 'Purple Rain', 9 Maurice and Robin, 10 The Sex Pistols.

Round 114 1 'Vanity Fair', 2 H Rider Haggard, 3 'The Catcher in the Rye', 4 'The Swiss Family Robinson', 5 Jay Gatsby in 'The Great Gatsby', 6 'The Call of the Wild', 7 'Harry Potter', 8 '2001: A Space Odyssey', 9 Sancho Panza, 10 Harry Palmer.

Round 115 1 Tasmania, 2 Denmark, 3 Sri Lanka, 4 Australia, 5 Sardinia, 6 Lesbos, 7 Cuba, 8 Cyprus, 9 Hokkaido, 10 Solomon.

Round 116 1 Maryland, 2 Paris, 3 The Netherlands, 4 Kimberley, 5 Honshu, 6 Florence, 7 Jordan, 8 Iberia, 9 Cook Strait, 10 Morocco.

Round 117 1 Richard Burton, 2 Nothing (the S is merely an initial), 3 Thomas Gray, 4 'Madame Butterfly', 5 'The Two Gentlemen of Verona', 6 A gaggle, 7 Frost, 8 Tennessee Williams, 9 Mozart, 10 'Frankenstein'.

Round 118 1 Daphne Du Maurier, 2 Thomas Stearns, 3 Jim Hawkins, 4 Sherlock Holmes, 5 'Macbeth', 6 Truman Capote, 7 Rabbits, 8 Leonard Cohen, 9 Roald Dahl, 10 Graham Greene.

Round 119   1 Roy Rogers, 2 Roger Moore, 3 The Twist, 4 Edward Stratemeyer, 5 'Coppélia', 6 Italy, 7 Claudette Colbert, 8 Goldie Hawn, 9 Cancan, 10 Terry Gilliam.

Round 120   1 Long-sightedness, 2 Plasma, 3 Aorta, 4 The skull, 5 A kidney, 6 Ribs, 7 Bones, 8 The leg (calf), 9 12, 10 The epiglottis.

Round 121   1 Hawaiian Islands, 2 First to fly non-stop across the Atlantic Ocean, 3 Liberia, 4 Wales, 5 Hurricane force, 6 Libretto, 7 Three, 8 Osama bin Laden, 9 The Duma, 10 Six.

Round 122   1 Boston, 2 Sir Martin Frobisher, 3 Jutes, 4 Aborigines, 5 Neil Armstrong, 6 Janet Reno, 7 Incas, 8 Brigham Young, 9 South Africa, 10 Ivan Boesky.

Round 123   1 Erich Honecker, 2 John F Kennedy, 3 China's emperors, 4 Prohibition, 5 Gerald Ford, 6 Iceland, 7 Australia, 8 Benazir Bhutto, 9 Bob Hoskins, 10 John Warner.

Round 124   1 FloJo, 2 Wayne Gretzky, 3 Jean-Claude Killy, 4 'Airplane', 5 Michael Owen, 6 Cassius Clay, 7 Evonne Goolagong, 8 The Melbourne Cup, 9 'Magic', 10 Giuseppe Farina.

Round 125   1 Elizabeth I, 2 Circle of animals, 3 Capricorn, 4 Four books, 5 Iraq, 6 Account of the stars, 7 Born on the cusp, 8 Nancy Reagan, 9 30, 10 The Sun.

Round 126   1 Man-made plastic, 2 Emily Davison, 3 Seahorses, 4 Lucifer, 5 Hermes, 6 The angel rulers/guardians of planets, 7 Quail, 8 Death, 9 Figure skating, 10 Champagne.

Round 127   1 Puccini, 2 Engine 49, 3 'Unchain My Heart', 4 Joan Armatrading, 5 Frédéric Chopin, 6 AC/DC, 7 'Porgy and Bess', 8 Siouxsie and the Banshees, 9 U2, 10 Mozart.

ANSWERS

Round 128   1 Iraq, 2 Congo, 3 St Lawrence, 4 Mediterranean, 5 Danube, 6 Shannon, 7 Caspian, 8 Rio Grande, 9 Buenos Ares and Montevideo, 10 Russia.

Round 129   1 Merle Haggard, 2 Wild Bill Hickok, 3 The Boston Strangler, 4 Butch Cassidy, 5 Frank, 6 Legs Diamond, 7 Patty Hearst, 8 A garage, 9 2 The Smiths, 10 The Unabomber.

Round 130   1 A diamond, 2 Numbat, 3 Sloth, 4 Toga, 5 Random House, 6 XIX, 7 Snakes, 8 650, 9 Dalmatian, 10 Conga.

Round 131   1 Diana Ross, 2 Martin Campbell, 3 Annette Bening, 4 Meryl Streep, 5 Charlie Chaplin, 6 Elizabeth Hurley, 7 'Mississippi Burning', 8 Kenneth Branagh, 9 Rex Harrison, 10 'A League of Their Own'.

Round 132   1 Geese, 2 Permafrost, 3 Mirage, 4 Mandible, 5 Carbon dioxide, 5 Snow leopard, 6 Lightning conductor, 8 Aardvark, 9 New Zealand, 10 Sargasso Sea.

Round 133   1 Salome, 2 Pestilence, War, Famine and Death, 3 Solomon, 4 969 years, 5 Sodom and Gomorrah, 6 Simon Peter, 7 Jacob, 8 Lazarus, 9 Five, 10 The meek.

Round 134   1 James I, 2 Vesuvius, 3 Yugoslavia, 4 Iceland, 5 Joseph McCarthy, 6 Ayatollah Khomeini, 7 Hong Kong, 8 Turkey, 9 Newfoundland, 10 1492.

Round 135   1 Poland, 2 White, 3 Six, 4 One sixteenth, 5 Portugal, 6 Arthur C. Clarke's, 7 Sicily, 8 Bucharest, 9 8, 10 Argentina (República Argentina in Spanish).

Round 136   1 Albrecht Duerer, 2 'The Scream', 3 Frans Hals, 4 Hieronymus Bosch, 5 Gare d'Orsay, 6 Van Gogh, 7 David, 8 Edgar Degas, 9 Caspar David Friedrich, 10 Blue Rider.

ANSWERS

Round 137   1 Lake Geneva, 2 Cook Strait, 3 Hartford, 4 Somalia, 5 Chicago, 6 Zürich, 7 Czech Republic, 8 Lake Huron, 9 Mexico, 10 Ohio.

Round 138   1 Thermodynamics, 2 The Ohm, 3 Gas, liquid, solid, 4 The Newton, 5 Lens, 6 Absolute zero, 7 Cold fusion, 8 Kelvin, 9 Viscosity, 10 Newton's.

Round 139   1 Botswana, 2 Frets, 3 Danish, 4 Italy, 5 Japanese, 6 Brazil, 7 Henrik Ibsen, 8 Spike, 9 Valhalla, 10 Damien Hirst.

Round 140   1 Aaron Copland, 2 Peter Tchaikovsky, 3 Leo Delibes, 4 Sergei Prokofiev, 5 Igor Stravinsky, 6 Claude Debussy, 7 Manuel de Falla, 8 Frederic Chopin, 9 Mozart, 10 'The Nutcracker'.

Round 141   1 'Titanic', 2 Short Take Off and Landing, 3 The 'Mayflower', 4 'Cannonball', 5 Tea, 6 The Kiel Canal, 7 A knot, 8 Caravan, 9 Barents Sea, 10 Tower Bridge.

Round 142   1 Maria Sharapova, 2 Women's badminton, 3 Nadia Comaneci, 4 1994-95, 5 On the bars (uneven or horizontal), 6 Spain, 7 The Pan American Games, 8 Canada, 9 Ingemar Johansson, 10 The Green Bay Packers.

Round 143   1 Katie, 2 Ray Bradbury, 3 Petruchio, 4 John Le Carré, 5 John Gay, 6 Cardinal Richelieu, 7 Joel Chandler Harris, 8 David Mamet, 9 Arthur Miller, 10 'The Tempest'.

Round 144   1 Toledo, 2 Physical evidence of UFOs, 3 Darkness, 4 Dutch, 5 The first regular newspaper, 6 Italian, 7 Who Dares Wins, 8 Terry Anderson, 9 Garrotte, 10 From behind.

Round 145   1 Fins, 2 Fiddler crab, 3 Goose, 4 Sepia, 5 Puff adder, 6 Bird, 7 Ticks, 8 Vixen, 9 Cats, 10 Africa.

ANSWERS

Round 146 1 Executive Mansion, 2 The Red Baron, 3 The Chattanooga Choo Choo, 4 Ronald Reagan, 5 Bill Clinton, 6 Claudius, 7 St Helena, 8 U.S.A. and Canada, 9 Bolivia, 10 Truman.

Round 147 1 Leander, 2 Adonis, 3 Saturnalia, 4 Clytemnestra, 5 Clio, 6 Daphne, 7 Zeus, 8 Hydra, 9 Unicorn, 10 Cerberus.

Round 148 1 Dennis Wilson, 2 South Dakota, 3 Valparaiso, 4 High fashion, 5 Baccarat, 6 Italy, 7 Mantilla, 8 German, 9 Cry from the heart, 10 Alma mater.

Round 149 1 Giuseppe Garibaldi, 2 Kuwait, 3 Wernher von Braun, 4 Stonewall, 5 'Never So Few', 6 Romania, 7 Spandau, 8 Pershing, 9 Neutron bomb, 10 Battle of the Bulge.

Round 150 1 A Manhattan, 2 Parmesan, 3 Pepperoni, 4 Socrates, 5 Portugal, 6 Sicily, 7 Spinach, 8 Rice, 9 Gluten, 10 Sushi.

Round 151 1 'Shogun', 2 'Move Over, Darling', 3 'The Mighty', 4 'Riot', 5 'Raising Arizona', 6 River Phoenix, 7 'A Low Down Dirty Shame', 8 Anne Heche, 9 Vicki Baum, 10 Cate Blanchett.

Round 152 1 The Everly Brothers, 2 'Forbidden', 3 Jon Bon Jovi, 4 David Bowie, 5 Cher, 6 Eric Clapton, 7 'The Dance', 8 Tom Jones, 9 The B52s, 10 Diana Ross.

Round 153 1 U.S.A. and Britain, 2 A newspaper, 3 Sun, 4 Kangaroo, 5 'Robin Hood, Prince of Thieves', 6 Ethiopia, 7 Garcia, 8 Clark Gable, 9 'Eroica', 10 Iberian.

Round 154 1 Michael Moorcock, 2 'Minority Report', 3 Arthur C Clarke, 4 'Cat's Cradle,' 5 J. G. Ballard, 6 Brian Aldiss, 7 'Dune', 8 'A Canticle for Leibowitz', 9 John Wyndham, 10 'The Death of Grass'.

Round 155 1 Italian, 2 Latin, 3 Alliteration, 4 India, 5 Greek, 6 Spanish, 7 Yiddish, 8 Bungalow, 9 St. Cyril, 10 Finland.

Round 156 1 Nylon, 2 Alexander Fleming, 3 Physics, 4 Smallpox, 5 Diuretics, 6 Tungsten, 7 Cardiology, 8 Minim, 9 Urticaria, 10 Philadelphia.

Round 157 1 Agatha Christie, 2 Belgium, 3 'Vanity Fair', 4 Popeye the Sailor Man, 5 Hungary, 6 California, 7 Strategic Defense Initiative, 8 Bip, 9 A type of stork, 10 Manitoba.

Round 158 1 John Lennon, 2 The first solo ascent without using oxygen, 3 Desert Fox, 4 Leon Trotsky, 5 Pol Pot, 6 Henry II, 7 Dallas, 8 The Battle of Trafalgar, 9 Vietnam, 10 Richard Nixon.

Round 159 1 Europe (Spain), 2 Salisbury, 3 Greece, 4 South Africa, 5 Sicily, 6 Denver, 7 Alaska, 8 Appenines, 9 Mali, 10 Arctic.

Round 160 1 Charlemagne, 2 Saul, 3 Brigham Young, 4 St. Ignatius Loyola, 5 Moses, 6 Shinto, 7 Jesse, 8 Cain, 9 Moses, 10 St. Jude.

Round 161 1 General James Wolfe, 2 Mongols, 3 Croesus, 4 William McKinley, 5 Georges Clemenceau, 6 Chiang Kai-shek, 7 Indonesia, 8 Julius Caesar, 9 Fidel Castro, 10 Argentina.

Round 162 1 Sexual relations, 2 Hydra, 3 Strait of Magellan, 4 Meteor showers, 5 Ambrose Bierce, 6 New York, 7 Jupiter, 8 The U.S.A., 9 Muttley, 10 Westerns.

Round 163 1 Discus, 2 Jesse Owens, 3 Figure skating, 4 Katarina Witt, 5 Lillehammer, 6 St Louis, 7 Greece, 8 Olympiad, 9 Muhammad Ali, 10 1996.

Round 164 1 Hungary, 2 Florida, 3 Lake Ontario, 4 Lake Erie, 5 Interlaken, 6 Finland, 7 Lake Titicaca, 8 Lake Ontario, 9 Geneva, 10 The Aral Sea.

Round 165   1 Overture, 2 Terpsichorean, 3 Two, 4 Woodstock, 5 Violin ('The Red Violin'), 6 Guitar, 7 Violins, 8 Harp, 9 Junior Walker, 10 Robin Williams.

Round 166   1 William Herschel, 2 DeForest Kelley, 3 Iceland, 4 North Sea, 5 Percival Lowell, 6 'Salome', 7 'Faust', 8 Murray river, 9 Isis, 10 Silver.

Round 167   1 Sodium, 2 Palladium, 3 Vernier, 4 Red, 5 Ballistics, 6 Humidity, 7 Stephen Hawking, 8 America Online, 9 Andrei Sakharov, 10 Astatine.

Round 168   1 Molière, 2 'Dr. Zhivago', 3 George Orwell, 4 Sir John Tenniel, 5 Jeanette Winterson, 6 Ogden Nash, 7 'The Swiss Family, Robinson', 8 Friday, 9 Dashiell Hammet, 10 Nevil Shute.

Round 169   1 Jimmy Durante, 2 Mouse, 3 Muppets, 4 U.S.A., 5 "Open sesame", 6 Django Reinhardt, 7 Woody Woodpecker, 8 John Steinbeck, 9 'You've Got Mail', 10 Charlie 'Bird' Parker.

Round 170   1 1789, 2 St. Helena, 3 1812, 4 Jimmy Carter, 5 South Africa, 6 1961, 7 Haiti, 8 Queen Victoria, 9 Kittyhawk, 10 Sarajevo.

Round 171   1 Woody Allen, 2 Aladdin, 3 Don Juan, 4 Algeria, 5 Hudson Bay, 6 Australia, 7 Sunflower, 8 Voltaire, 9 Avenue of the Americas, 10 Crystal gazing.

Round 172   1 Barbra Streisand, 2 Jodie Foster, 3 '48 Hrs', 4 Dustin Hoffman, 5 'The Horseman on the Roof', 6 Kyle Maclachlan, 7 Alfred Hitchcock, 8 'Snow White and the Seven Dwarfs', 9 Mike Myers, 10 Daphne du Maurier.

Round 173   1 Valhalla, 2 Dionysus, 3 Medusa, 4 Androcles, 5 Eurydice, 6 The Holy Grail, 7 His heel, 8 Romulus and Remus, 9 Chimaera, 10 Phoenix.

Round 174 1 John Constable, 2 Giotto, 3 Eric Gill, 4 'The Blue Boy', 5 Swiss, 6 Post-Impressionism, 7 Aubrey Beardsley, 8 Georges Seurat, 9 Rembrandt, 10 Crete.

Round 175 1 Aristophanes, 2 The Falklands War, 3 Louisville, Kentucky, 4 Tibet, 5 The Silk Road, 6 Ho Chi Minh, 7 Germaine Greer, 8 Ernest Shackleton, 9 Germany, 10 Coral Sea.

Round 176 1 Caspar Weinberger, 2 Hungary, 3 New Zealand, 4 President Gerald Ford, 5 Iran, 6 35, 7 Midway, 8 'The Washington Post', 9 Richard Nixon, 10 Davy Crockett.

Round 177 1 Venice, 2 England, 3 United States, 4 Germany, 5 Czechoslovakia, 6 Ghanaian, 7 Brazil, 8 Poland, 9 Denmark, 10 England.

Round 178 1 Gioacchino Rossini, 2 Ottorino Respighi, 3 Maurice Ravel, 4 'The Wilis', 5 Vaughan Williams, 6 'Gayaneh', 7 'The Nutcracker', 8 'Petrouchka', 9 Finnish, 10 'Moonlight'.

Round 179 1 Borzoi, 2 Lizard, 3 A Dutch barge dog, 4 Swan, 5 Ants, 6 Albatross, 7 Condor, 8 A killer whale, 9 Pearls, 10 Tibet.

Round 180 1 Corazon, 2 Russia, 3 Burma (or Myanmar), 4 North Korea, 5 The Verve, 6 Camp David, 7 Methane, 8 The U. S. A., 9 St. Petersburg, 10 The Globe.

Round 181 1 Lourdes, 2 Ligurian Sea, 3 Cape Town, 4 The Sahara, 5 North face, 6 Florida, 7 Cape Horn, 8 The Nile, 9 The Amazon, 10 Ceylon.

Round 182 1 Ice hockey, 2 Cycling, 3 Baseball, 4 The America's Cup, 5 Rookie, 6 Ice-skating, 7 Basketball, 8 Lacrosse, 9 Tennis, 10 Ty Cobb.

Round 183 1 John Wycliffe, 2 Salome, 3 Thirty, 4 A golden calf, 5 Revelation, 6 Mount Ararat, 7 Thorns and thistles, 8 Aaron's, 9 The jaw-bone of an ass, 10 Ten.

Round 184 1 Greece, 2 Morocco, 3 Cirrus, 4 Guatemala, 5 Veneer, 6 Paris, 7 Maine, 8 Orlando, 9 Devil's Tower, 10 'Star'.

Round 185 1 Kamikaze, 2 Mungo Park, 3 Troy, 4 Yuri Gagarin, 5 Chicago, 6 John Boyd Dunlop, 7 Californian gold miners, 8 Austria and Russia, 9 Electronic computer, 10 The machine gun.

Round 186 1 Al Capone, 2 Alibi, 3 Bonnie and Clyde, 4 The Birdman of Alcatraz, 5 New York, 6 District Attorney, 7 Charles, 8 Jesse James, 9 Machine-Gun, 10 The Wailers.

Round 187 1 Yitzhak Rabin, 2 Pope John Paul II, 3 Memphis, 4 Macbeth, 5 Anwar Sadat, 6 Indira and Rajiv, 7 Abraham Lincoln, 8 Iraq, 9 Lord Louis Mountbatten, 10 Sweden.

Round 188 1 Charles Lindbergh, 2 'Bluebird', 3 Panama Canal, 4 Sweden, 5 General Motors, 6 Alcock and Brown, 7 Austrian, 8 Caravelle, 9 Wiley Post, 10 Fiat.

Round 189 1 German, 2 Air force, 3 Munich, 4 Jim Henson, 5 Maya, 6 Chinoiserie, 7 Aircraft carriers, 8 Madras, 9 Maine, 10 Arnold Schwarzenegger.

Round 190 1 Steely Dan, 2 Simple Minds, 3 The Who, 4 'Faith', 5 'Thriller', 6 UB40, 7 'Ray of Light', 8 Men at Work, 9 Don McLean's 'American Pie', 10 Jethro Tull.

Round 191 1 Collar bone, 2 The hand, 3 The liver, 4 Malaria, 5 The ear, 6 Beriberi, 7 The liver, 8 Acne, 9 Mumps, 10 Placenta.

Round 192 1 'Murder in the First', 2 Clint Eastwood, 3 'The Santa Clause', 4 Andy Warhol ('I Shot Andy Warhol'), 5 Peggy Ashcroft, 6 'The American President', 7 Peter Ustinov, 8 Harrison Ford, 9 Mack Sennett, 10 The Lone Ranger.

Round 193   1 American Airlines and United Airlines, 2 Karl Marx, 3 Broadway, New York, 4 IKEA, 5 Wendi Deng, 6 Russia, 7 Jelly Roll Morton, 8 Crabs, 9 Marco Polo, 10 Guitar.

Round 194   1 Samuel Beckett, 2 'Mary Poppins', 3 William Trevor, 4 Sir Henry Newbolt, 5 Juvenal, 6 H.E. Bates, 7 'Gone with the Wind', 8 'The Odyssey', 9 'Gentlemen Marry Brunettes', 10 'Alice Through The Looking Glass'.

Round 195   1 Hungary, 2 Okra, 3 Brazil, 4 Clementine, 5 Chicken-a-la-King, 6 Retinol, 7 Caffeine, 8 Bordeaux, 9 Orange, 10 Glycerine.

Round 196   1 Lady Macbeth, 2 Athens, 3 Montague and Capulet, 4 Shylock, 5 Macbeth, 6 'The Tempest', 7 Titania, 8 'Twelfth Night', 9 'Measure for Measure', 10 Desdemona.

Round 197   1 Anthropology, 2 Betty Ford, 3 Swastika, 4 Donald Woods, 5 Calamity Jane, 6 Erwin Rommel, 7 Alan Shepard, 8 The Hanging Gardens of Babylon, 9 Portuguese, 10 Television.

Round 198   1 George Eastman, 2 Isobar, 3 Dutch, 4 Halifax, 5 'New World', 6 Cancer, 7 Cullinan, 8 Parkinson's Law, 9 The number 13, 10 Zurich.

Round 199   1 They made the 'Black Power Salute', 2 Maureen Connolly, 3 Spa, 4 Liechtenstein, 5 1964, 6 New York Cosmos, 7 Ascari, 8 Bernhard Langer, 9 Silverstone, England, 10 He refused military conscription.

Round 200   1 Argentina, 2 J. Robert Oppenheimer, 3 My Lai, 4 France, 5 Jane Fonda, 6 Manhattan, 7 'The Thin Red Line', 8 Dixie, 9 Nuremberg, 10 International Red Cross.

Round 201   1 Ceres, 2 Benjamin Franklin, 3 Vinegar, 4 Observatory, 5 Cement, 6 Speleology, 7 Barometer, 8 Michael Faraday, 9 Plaster of Paris, 10 Streamlining.

Round 202   1 Nine, 2 'Of Mice and Men', 3 David Lean, 4 South Africa, 5 Storm petrel, 6 Lesbos, 7 Muezzin, 8 Lima, 9 Faux pas, 10 Bantam.

Round 203   1 Hawaii, 2 The Pyrenees, 3 Aegean Sea, 4 Rotterdam, 5 Madagascar, 6 Abel Tasman, 7 Europe, 8 The Mediterranean, 9 Mauritius, 10 Niagara.

Round 204   1 Miles Davis, 2 Buddy 'Kid' Bolden, 3 Wm. 'Count' Basie, 4 Wm. 'Bunk' Johnson, 5 'Whalemouth', 6 Sidney Bechet, 7 Joseph 'King' Oliver, 8 Ferdinand 'Jelly Roll' Morton, 9 Clarinet, 10 'Sweet and Lowdown'.

Round 205   1 Haiti, 2 Rockall, 3 Denmark, 4 Portugal, 5 Florida, 6 The Adriatic, 7 Cuba, 8 Norway, 9 Alaska, 10 Madeira.

Round 206   1 Mars and Jupiter, 2 Saturn, 3 The Sun, 4 Hawaii, 5 Orion, 6 Gemini, 7 John Glenn, 8 First American woman in space, 9 Skylab, 10 Orion.

Round 207   1 Canary Islands, 2 Frisbee, 3 Czechoslovakia, 4 First overland transit of Antarctica, 5 Eyes, 6 Julius Caesar, 7 Bison, 8 Jordan, 9 Odin, 10 Brazil.

Round 208   1 Baal, 2 Hinduism, 3 Christianity, 4 Hare Krishna, 5 Heaven's Gate, 6 The Baha'i Faith, 7 Medina, 8 Phylacteries, 9 The Ganges, 10 Ethiopia.

Round 209   1 Douglas MacArthur, 2 Rasputin, 3 Vaslav, 4 Louis XV, 5 Appian Way, 6 The Black Death, 7 Howard Hughes, 8 Amerigo Vespucci, 9 Decimation, 10 Louis XIV.

Round 210   1 Robert Frost, 2 154, 3 Lord Byron, 4 'The Owl and the Pussycat', 5 Percy Shelley, 6 'Hero', 7 'Sea Fever', 8 Beat poetry, 9 'Jerusalem', 10 'The Raven'.

ANSWERS

Round 211   1 Japan, 2 Germany, 3 Havelock Ellis, 4 Lisbon, 5 St Swithin,
6 The Falkland Islands, 7 Mongolia, 8 Anarchy, 9 'The Tempest„
10 Stockholm.

Round 212   1 Berlin (Philharmonic), 2 Harold Arlen, 3 Tarzan, 4 Errol Flynn,
5 Beethoven, 6 Beagle, 7 A bird, 8 Cousin, 9 Cleveland, 10 Sharks
and Jets.

Round 213   1 Eucalyptus, 2 Tsetse fly, 3 African, 4 Ergot, 5 Cedar of Lebanon,
6 Zoology, 7 Lobster, 8 Hare, 9 Giraffe, 10 Australia.

Round 214   1 Argo, 2 Thor, 3 Narcissus, 4 Capture it, 5 Cyclops, 6 Earth,
7 Friday (Freya), 8 Aurora, 9 Harpy, 10 Achilles.

Round 215   1 Dr. McCoy, 2 Martin Scorsese, 3 Andie MacDowell, 4 Holly
Golightly, 5 O.J. Simpson, 6 'The Brothers McMullen', 7 Woody
Allen, 8 Sam Spade, 9 'Calamity Jane', 10 Frankie Avalon.

Round 216   1 'Beau Geste„ 2 The mistral, 3 Trees, 4 Demography, 5 Florence
Nightingale, 6 New York, 7 Muslin, 8 Denim, 9 The Parthenon,
10 Yellow.

Round 217   1 Patsy Cline, 2 Russia, 3 Andrés Segovia, 4 Joseph, 5 Johann the
Younger, 6 Salzburg, 7 Squeeze, 4 Bruce Springsteen, 9 Johnny
Dankworth, 10 Thomas 'Fats' Waller.

Round 218   1 7.32 metres (eight yards), 2 Miami Beach, South America 3,
4 The Baltimore Ravens, 5 Hand-cycling, 6 Turkey, 7 12, 8 Surfing,
9 Ulaanbaatar, 10 Manning Field.

Round 219   1 Gustave Flaubert, 2 Beelzebub, 3 Irwin Shaw, 4 Henrik Ibsen,
5 Edward Fitzgerald, 6 Fourteen, 7 'Frankenstein', 8 Maya Angelou,
9 Gladstone, 10 Bonn.

Round 220 1 Rome, 2 Spanish Flu, 3 'Bright Eyes', 4 John Keats, 5 Electric guitar, 6 Magnitude, 7 Obsidian, 8 Words, 9 The Suez and Panama Canals, 10 Wensleydale.

Round 221 1 Alexander Graham Bell, 2 General Gordon, 3 Singapore, 4 Giuseppe Verdi, 5 Cornwallis, 6 Josef Stalin, 7 Los Angeles, 8 Mikhail Gorbachev, 9 The light bulb, 10 Winnie Mandela.

Round 222 1 Toronto, 2 Australia (Australis), 3 Uganda, 4 Lake Titicaca, 5 Albuquerque, 6 Karachi, 7 Hungary, 8 Estonia, 9 Venezuela, 10 Africa.

Round 223 1 Djibouti, 2 China, 3 Malawi, 4 France, 5 New Zealand, 6 Argentina, 7 South Africa, 8 Romania, 9 Morocco, 10 Jordan.

Round 224 1 Polk and Taft, 2 John Tyler, 3 Ronald Reagan, 4 John Tyler, 5 Abraham Lincoln, 6 James Buchanan, 7 Michael Dukakis, 8 Lyndon Johnson, 9 Harry S. Truman, 10 Abraham Lincoln.

Round 225 1 Franz Mesmer, 2 Zinc, 3 Vancouver, 4 Tin, 5 Aurora, 6 'Catch-22', 7 The Requiem, 8 John Philip Sousa, 9 Prehensile, 10 D-Day: the Allies' invasion of German-occupied France.

Round 226 1 Fuel injection, 2 Fallout, 3 Three Mile Island, 4 Stratosphere and Troposphere, 5 Foxglove, 6 Washing soda, 7 Kaleidoscope, 8 Inertia, 9 Menthol, 10 Actinides.

Round 227 1 Slavery, 2 Union of Soviet Socialist Republics, 2 Tamerlane, 3 Rajiv Gandhi, 5 Al Gore, 6 Harry S. Truman, 7 Israel, 8 Canada, 9 The Soviet Union, 10 William Henry Harrison.

Round 228 1 'Candid Camera', 2 Kristin Shepard, 3 The Cartwrights, 4 Larry Hagman, 5 George Wendt, 6 Principal Skinner, 7 'The Phil Silvers Show', 8 Sarah Michelle Gellar, 9 Cybill Shepherd, 10 'The Colbys'.

Round 229 1 Spaniel, 2 FBI, 3 Verey pistol, 4 Johanna Spyri, 5 Horse, 6 Euthanasia, 7 Red, 8 Windmills, 9 Palimony, 10 Hyena.

Round 230 1 'Swan Lake', 2 'Les Sylphides', 3 Diaghilev, 4 Prokofiev, 5 Anna Pavlova, 6 Nijinsky, 7 Two notes occupying the same time as a triplet, 8 Musical flourish with trumpets, 9 Russian, 10 Joseph Haydn.

Round 231 1 7, 2 3 (California, Colorado and Connecticut), 3 76, 4 1812, 5 99, 6 20,000, 7 12, 8 187, 9 72, 10 23.

Round 232 1 Calvin Coolidge, 2 Kaiser, 3 Peter Stuyvesant, 4 China, 5 Albania, 6 Peruvian, 7 John Alexander MacDonald, 8 Schicklgruber, 9 Saddam Hussein, 10 Golda Meir.

Round 233 1 Edward de Bono, 2 Peking man, 3 1889, 4 The Great Fire of London, 5 Princess Anastasia of Russia , 6 San Francisco, 7 Aretha Franklin, 8 Carnarvon, 9 London, 10 She gave birth to the first surviving sextuplets.

Round 234 1 Louis Armstrong, 2 Seamus Heaney, 3 Wood, 4 Don Quixote, 5 South Africa, 6 Gustave Doré, 7 Amerigo Vespucci, 8 Ostrich, 9 Green, 10 'Hindenburg'.

Round 235 'Ben Hur', 2 Orson Welles, 3 The Sundance Kid, 4 'The Shining', 5 'Galaxy Quest', 6 'Scream' 3, 7 Mel Gibson, 8 'Heroes', 9 Henry Fonda, 10 Nickelodeon.

Round 236 1 Sikhism, 2 Gothic, 3 'The Satanic Verses', 4 Karma, 5 Chile, 6 George Fox, 7 Mennonites, 8 St. Basil's, 9 Trappist, 10 Notre-Dame de Paris.

Round 237 1 Ice hockey, 2 Stanley Matthews, 3 Ty Cobb, 4 The Brown Bomber, 5 Greg Norman, 6 Javelin, 7 Billie Jean King, 8 Squash, 9 Bradford, 10 Long-distance running.

ANSWERS

Round 238 1 Chicago, 2 Monkey, 3 Samuel Hahnemann, 4 Sagittarius, 5 Neil Simon, 6 Leo, 7 RADAR, 8 Willow, 9 Cactus, 10 Hair.

Round 239 1 Saluki, 2 South America, 3 Monkey, 4 Pig, 5 Camels, 6 Gills, 7 Possum (or opossum), 8 Cougar, 9 Shellac, 10 Hind legs.

Round 240 1 Son of Sam, 2 Bragging, 3 Al Capone, 4 New York, 5 Pretty Boy, 6 John Mitchell, 7 Florence, 8 Fingerprints, 9 John Brown, 10 Haiti.

Round 241 1 Tortilla, 2 Genetically Modified, 3 Cos, 4 Pomegranate, 5 Potatoes, 6 Greece, 7 White Lady, 8 Durum, 9 Orange, 10 The sandwich (he was the 4th Earl of Sandwich).

Round 242 1 Jerry Goldsmith, 2 Maurice Jarre, 3 Henry Mancini, 4 John Barry, 5 Hans Zimmer, 6 Rachmaninoff, 7 '2001: A Space Odyssey', 8 'West Side Story', 9 Gustav Mahler, 10 'The Dollars' trilogy.

Round 243 1 Venice, 2 Bohemia, 3 Sirius, 4 Arcturus, 5 Scandinavia, 6 The ear, 7 Migraine, 8 Cadfael, 9 '1812 Overture', 10 Australia.

Round 244 1 Stromboli, 2 Dardanelles, 3 Glastonbury, 4 Naples, 5 Prague, 6 Spain, 7 China, 8 Khartoum, 9 Honolulu, 10 Tunisia.

Round 245 1 Desert Storm, 2 Turin, 3 Lisbon, 4 Potato, 5 A dance, 6 The Philippines, 7 The alarm clock, 8 Vaseline, 9 The Taj Mahal, 10 The Angel Falls (the world's highest waterfall).

Round 246 1 'Hamlet,' 2 J.R.R. Tolkien, 3 Tom Stoppard, 4 Nova Scotia, 5 Joseph Heller, 6 Saul Bellow, 7 Max Weber, 8 Octavio Paz, 9 A swan, 10 Christopher Robin.

Round 247 1 'West Side Story', 2 Canaries, 3 Canada, 4 Iceland, 5 Fred Hoyle, 6 'A Christmas Carol', 7 Throat, 8 Africa, 9 Gene Roddenberry, 10 'Nineteen Eighty-Four'.

ANSWERS

Round 248 1 New York City, 2 Diego Velazquez, 3 Juan Gris, 4 His mother, 5 Damien Hirst, 6 Henry VIII, 7 Grandson, 8 Russia, 9 Van Gogh, 10 Finnish.

Round 249 1 Florence, 2 Italy, 3 New York, 4 The Alps, 5 Sydney Harbour Bridge, 6 Prague, 7 Denmark, 8 Venice, 9 Rocky Mountains, 10 Louisiana.

Round 250 1 Velodrome, 2 Pawn, 3 Spain, 4 Joe Frazier, 5 Vanderbilt, 6 Orenthal James, 7 Advantage, 8 Roscoe Tanner, 9 Eddie Lawson, 10 Diabolo.

Round 251 1 The nose, 2 The iris, 3 Dyslexia, 4 Anaesthesia, 5 Finger movement, 6 Amniocentesis, 7 Chromosomes, 8 The ear, 9 Frostbite, 10 The pulmonary artery.

Round 252 1 A sundial, 2 Canada, 3 Pelham Grenville, 4 Armies, 5 Terror and Fear, 6 'Oh Come All Ye Faithful', 7 A bat, 8 Adolf Hitler, 9 Manhattan, 10 Copenhagen.

Round 253 1 Four, 2 'The Three Sisters', 3 Sergeant York, 4 Daddy Warbucks, 5 A year and a day, 6 Sam Malone, 7 'Hamlet', 8 Charlton Heston, 9 Gardenia, 10 Vulcan.

Round 254 1 David Bowie, 2 AC/DC, 3 Spandau Ballet, 4 Donna Summer, 5 The Pointer Sisters, 6 Frank Zappa, 7 The Who, 8 Van Halen, 9 Robert Cray, 10 Crosby, Stills, Nash and Young.

Round 255 1 'Dr. Jekyll and Ms. Hyde', 2 'Torn Curtain', 3 Peter O'Toole, 4 'The Tie That Binds', 5 Keanu Reeves, 6 Tina Turner, 7 'Jumanji', 8 Paul Newman, 9 Boris Karloff's, 10 Kelly McGillis.

Round 256 1 Citric, 2 Nero, 3 Helsinki, 4 New York, 5 Lintel, 6 J Edgar Hoover, 7 No. 4, 8 Francis Ford Coppola, 9 South Africa, 10 Rome.

Round 257 1 August (31st), 2 Mother Teresa, 3 'Arbeit Macht Frei', 4 Quebec, 5 Salt Lake City, 6 Chaka (or Shaka), 7 Iran, 8 Nicolae Ceausescu of Romania, 9 Black Monday, 10 Paul Revere.

Round 258 1 Mr Ed, 2 'Benson', 3 'Cheers', 4 Lisa Kudrow, 5 Sunshine Cab Company, 6 'The Munsters', 7 Waylon, 8 'Bewitched', 9 'The Cosby Show', 10 'Arrested Development'.

Round 259 1 Gawain, 2 Ares, 3 Jason, 4 Pegasus, 5 Excalibur, 6 Hypnos, 7 Neptune, 8 Andromache, 9 Venus, 10 Thursday (Thor).

Round 260 1 The Blue Mosque, 2 Pompidou, 3 Kuala Lumpur, 4 St. Petersburg, 5 Chicago, 6 The CN Tower, 7 Vienna, 8 Dubai, 9 Agra, 10 The Flatiron Building.

Round 261 1 Chop suey, 2 The S. S., 3 Charon, 4 Spinach, 5 Sinbad, 6 Titans, 7 Libya, 8 Hector, 9 Tam o' Shanter, 10 The Bridge of Sighs.

Round 262 1 Stevie Wonder, 2 Aerosmith, 3 Earth, Wind and Fire, 4 Billy Joel, 5 Mike Oldfield, 6 Pink Floyd, 7 The Rolling Stones, 8 The Lovin' Spoonful, 9 'The Rise and Fall of Ziggy Stardust and the Spiders From Mars', 10 The Carpenters.

Round 263 1 Quadrant, 2 Hydrometer, 3 Morphine, 4 Igneous, sedimentary and metamorphic, 5 Seveso, 6 Coulomb, 7 Intercontinental ballistic missile, 8 Refraction, 9 The cause of a disease or of a condition, 10 Magnetron.